When a
Woman
Overcomes
Life's Hurts

CINDI McMENAMIN

HARVEST HOUSE PUBLISHERS
EUGENE, OREGON

Cover by Dugan Design Group, Bloomington, Minnesota

Cover photo © ZenShui / Laurence Mouton / PhotoAlto Agency RF Collections / Getty Images

WHEN A WOMAN OVERCOMES LIFE'S HURTS
Copyright © 2012 by Cindi McMenamin
Published by Harvest House Publishers
Eugene, Oregon 97402
www.harvesthousepublishers.com

Library of Congress Cataloging-in-Publication Data
McMenamin, Cindi, 1965-
When a woman overcomes life's hurts / Cindi McMenamin.
p. cm.
Includes bibliographical references (p.   ).
ISBN 978-0-7369-4858-6 (pbk.)
ISBN 978-0-7369-4859-3 (eBook)
1. Christian women—Religious life. 2. Consolation. 3. Suffering—Religious aspects—
Christianity. 4. Pain—Religious aspects—Christianity. I. Title.
BV4527.M43275 2012
248.8'43—dc23

2011045883

12 13 14 15 16 17 18 19 20 / VP-CD / 10 9 8 7 6 5 4 3 2 1

For the precious women who have shared their pain in the pages of this book. You, my friends, are living examples of the healing and wholeness that only God can provide.

And for every woman who picks up this book seeking to overcome life's hurts—
my prayer is that you will come face-to-face with the Gentle Healer who has been waiting to turn your brokenness into something absolutely beautiful.

Acknowledgments

My heartfelt thanks to…

- my husband, Hugh, and daughter, Dana, for their unconditional love for me.

- my brother, Dan, for his ability to look beyond my wounds and focus on the transforming work God continues to do in me.

- my friends and partners in prayer who have upheld me through the writing of yet another book: Chris Castillero, Cyndi Evans, Theresa Fusco, Sue Laird, Cyndie Lester, Allison Martin, Lisa Pacheco, Debbie Patrick, Mary Purviance, Terri Smalls, Ashley Tarr, and Barbara Willett.

- my editor, Steve Miller, and the publisher's committee at Harvest House Publishers for believing in the need for this book.

And above all, I'm grateful to my Lord and Savior Jesus Christ, who did what it took so you and I could be whole and complete.

Contents

Rising Above the Hurts

Wouldn't it be wonderful to be able to say, "My life has turned out *exactly* the way I dreamed!"?

I suppose if you could say that, you'd be in heaven—literally.

But maybe, instead, you feel like you've been through hell.

Perhaps you've struggled with—or are still struggling through—a painful childhood, a broken relationship, a bitter divorce, the loss of someone you loved, the devastation of a dream, the diagnosis of a disease, or the deep disappointment that comes when life takes a sudden turn you didn't want or expect.

The wounds in life abound. And sometimes they are compounded, one upon the other, making us wonder *What's going on?* and *What did I do to deserve this?* At times we ask "Where are You, God? Don't You care?" and "Why do I have to hurt like this?" Regardless of what your particular painful situation is, if you've struggled with the "Why?" questions, you are not alone.

From as far back as she can remember, Cyndi has seen death all around her. Tragic death. Unexpected death. Death that no one talked about or explained or acknowledged. There was a time when she began to wonder why her life included so much sorrow and tears.

Sharon looks back on her childhood and finds no one—*no one*—who wanted her or loved her. Her mother, who tried to kill her when she was just a year old, was sent to live in a psychiatric hospital. Her father resented her ever since, and abused her physically and sexually until her teenage years. Then she married and was diagnosed with an aggressive cancer shortly before her marriage ended. Sharon remembers days when she prayed to die in order to escape her physical, emotional, and spiritual pain, but believed God wouldn't let her die because she wasn't good enough to get into heaven.

Deanna grew up with a critical mother and a father who remained emotionally distant from her, only to discover later that they were her adoptive parents and her *real* story was a secret. Feeling for years that she had a shameful past no one was willing to talk about and that she was unwanted and unloved, she finally married and felt loved for the first time…until she discovered that her husband was having a long-time affair with her best friend. There were times when she felt like a walking ghost, numb to anyone and anything around her.

And Christina was raised to run from the law, learning at an early age to produce drugs to make money for and feed the habit of her drug-addicted mother. Foraging through dumpsters for food and taking care of her four younger siblings as a young preteen, she often wondered if she'd ever have a "normal" life—one she could at least talk about with others.

I have many more stories I could share. And all of these women would tell you today that there is a *reason* for the wounds they've experienced. Anyone who knows those women, too, will tell you that they are some of the most remarkable women they've ever known. Their pain led to their purpose. Their brokenness added to their beauty. Their suffering made them stronger. And they are no longer women who ask "Why?" Amazingly, too, they are no longer women who consider themselves wounded.

As I wrote this book, I didn't look for women who were spiritual giants and were making a significant difference in the world and then ask them about their past hurts. I started with the wounds. I asked around for women who had come from the worst of the worst. I wanted to hear the stories of women who had endured heartache and then somehow moved beyond life's hurts. And what I found as I talked with many of them was that—from their perspective—their disappointment, loss, and hurt wasn't nearly as significant as their deliverance. They were focused not on their frustrations but on their futures, not on their hurts but on helping others.

These women had endured pain, but their lives are now all about God's plan and purpose. They are examples of how God can take broken women just like you and me and turn them into beautiful women with a passion for life. So this book is not merely about dealing with heartache and wounds. It's about encouragement and inspiration and moving beyond life's hurts and heartaches and into a place of hope and purpose. It's about how *you* can overcome life's hurts and experience God's healing and wholeness, and how you can offer that same healing and wholeness to others.

I will share with you each of these women's stories—and the stories of many more—so you can meet women who have experienced pain and are still standing, only stronger, and with a passion and purpose they hadn't had before. They have overcome life's hurts, some of which you may have experienced yourself.

God has healing and wholeness for you, too—regardless of how your hurt originated. Whether you were the victim of someone else's wrongdoing, you experienced the humiliation of betrayal or abandonment, you suffered a heartache or many of them, or your wounds came from your own regrettable actions, there is a fountain of healing that flows for those who are willing to receive it. God offers healing to you and can bring purpose out of your pain.

Pain as a Part of Life

Let me start off, dear sister, by gently reminding you that pain is a part of life. I have sometimes even wondered if it's *more* prevalent in a woman's life. Maybe it's because, as women, we just tend to talk about pain more, to wear our hearts on our sleeves and allow ourselves to be more vulnerable. Maybe we need to sift through it, analyze the motive behind it, and strive to understand it, learn from it, and ultimately come up with a *reason* for it. Maybe it's because we hold higher expectations of others and crash lower when our dreams, especially in the area of love, are dashed.

From the deep ache of abandonment, rejection, or lost love to the sting of an insult from someone we considered a friend, we feel the pain of living, loving, and losing—sometimes from day to day. But oh, to be able to rise above what has scarred us and come out stronger, more confident, and more of a blessing to everyone who encounters us! Oh, to be able to say, "I trust that the Lover of my Soul had a purpose and a plan in all that I have experienced. And I can look back on His loving hand on my life and say He was there and He has brought me faithfully to wholeness today."

Over the past 25 years of sitting across the table from hurting women, hearing the sobs of countless broken hearts and struggling through difficult questions—and experiencing a few of the heart-wrenching difficulties they've talked about—I can tell you there *is* an answer. There *is* healing. And there *is* a way to come out from the darkness and into the light again.

Over the past year alone, I've had the privilege of hearing, firsthand, some incredible stories of women finding their purpose through their pain, their ministry through their misery, their dream through their difficulty. I've seen beauty, not bitterness, develop where there was once only fear and resentment. I've seen women come through the worst of the worst and be able to hold their heads high and say, "I am wounded no more"—not only as a fact but as a motto in life!

Do you want to be in that place, too? You can…if you are willing to walk with me through a journey of letting God heal your heart from the inside out.

I'll admit this is a book I didn't want to write because initially I didn't want to take the journey it would require. Who wants to revisit their wounds, remember past hurts, and offer them up to God, saying, "I know You knew about this and You allowed it, too, so do what You want in and through me and have Your way"? Who wants to see unresolved issues still hiding in the corners of their hearts and find places of insecurity from childhood hurts not fully surrendered to God? Not me!

No, I would've much rather focused on other women and their journeys through pain and healing and left my situation alone. But God doesn't work that way—at least that's the way it's been in my life. He wants me to learn the lessons first, to grieve with my girlfriends through the writing of this book, and to live out what I write about. He wants me to test the principles and see if they're true, to apply the advice I'm giving and make sure it works in my own life, too. And when it came to this book, He wanted me to walk through this journey—and face some of the issues where I'm still wounded but didn't want to admit it—so I could offer to Him what still holds me back and then walk out of that hurt and into a hope, healing, and more defined purpose than I knew before. He wanted that for me…so that I could, in turn, take *your* hand and walk with you through the process, right alongside you.

So, dear reader, I embark on this journey *with* you—a journey of looking at the many common wounds women experience and how to overcome them and move forward into a brighter future.

We will start by *uncovering the wounds* that may still affect you today—wounds like falling in love, only to be rejected or betrayed. Wounds like experiencing the sting of rejection, the ache of betrayal, or the disappointment of dashed dreams.

Once we've uncovered the wounds, we will *unravel the lies* that you may have believed through the years, like…

- I don't really matter in the scope of things.

- I'm undesirable, and no one will ever cherish me.

- I'm a disappointment because of the choices I've made.

- I'm incapable—I'll never amount to anything.

- I'm too messed up for God to ever use me.

Once we've confronted those lies with the truth, we will *unveil a new heart* that is focused on the One who was wounded for us and the life He offers us from His scars so we can do the same—offer life and hope to others out of the hurts we've endured. Finally, we'll grab hold of the restoration that God is waiting to do in your life to bring a beautiful purpose out of what was once bitter pain.

This book does not contain psychology, but what I call the "therapy of theology"—applying a correct understanding of who God is and letting that truth penetrate our pain and past issues and deliver us from the bondage that has been holding us back. I know it works. I've seen it work in the lives of countless women. And I've experienced it first-hand. And I know you can experience it, too.

So, if you're ready, so am I. Come alongside me on this journey as we look at how to be pulled up from the pit and healed of your hurts so that you are a woman who can hold your head up high and honestly say, with all confidence, "I am wounded no more."

I am *so* ready for that place in life. Aren't you?

PART I:

Uncovering the Wounds

He heals the brokenhearted
and binds up their wounds.

PSALM 147:3

This Wasn't Supposed to Happen

Realizing There's a Reason for Your Pain

Ivonne never imagined her life would turn out the way it has.

At 40 years old, she still lives alone, without the husband and children she had hoped to share her life with by now. But her life is full and running over with blessings because she was content to let God have *His* way with His plans and purposes for her life. And Ivonne *can* imagine just how different—and devastating—her life might be today if God had not intervened and brought her through to the other side.

Let me pull back the curtain on Ivonne's life so you can get a glimpse of what *your* Creator might have had in mind when He allowed you to suffer in the way that you have. Let me show you the first story of many in which it wasn't about the pain—it was about the purpose, and a divine plan for something more.

Ivonne is the daughter of two Mexican immigrants who migrated to Pasadena, California, when she was six years old. Their first few months in the United States were very difficult, so they traveled back to Mexico. A year later they tried the move again with many hardships—sleeping under a bridge in a car, or in a trailer park, or in one small room of a relative's home.

For the first four years after coming to the United States, Ivonne lived all over the Los Angeles area. "I attended four different schools from the age of 7 to 11. We had a very typical immigrant family experience. My parents worked full-time. I took care of my two younger siblings. We stayed home alone often. Our parents weren't very good stewards of their money, so at times we had what we needed and other times it seemed like we were being evicted every other month because we couldn't pay the rent. I spent two years living in a small bedroom in my uncle's house. My parents, sister, brother, and myself all shared one room."

During this time that Ivonne was left alone to care for her siblings, cousins, and grandparent, an older cousin of hers sexually molested her on two occasions.

"When I finally built up the courage to tell my parents about it, he was simply beaten up by the older uncles and cousins and 'shipped' back to Mexico. There was no therapy or counseling for me. I was expected to forget the whole thing, which I did...for a while."

Ivonne grew up in an extremely unstable environment. But she also learned how to cope and find joy in music, movies, laughter, and the close bond she shared with her sister and brother, a bond that continues to this day.

"At a young age, I began to feel that I would never have an ordinary life, that I was called to something bigger than my circumstances. As a child I didn't know what that meant or what it looked like. I just felt it. In retrospect, I know it was Jesus' hand on my life.

"When I was in eighth grade, the family discovered that my father was having an affair with his brother's wife, an aunt we had grown to love and depend on as a second mother. My mother was pregnant with my baby brother at the time. After months of threats that my parents would separate, my father came to me as I was getting ready for school one day and demanded that I tell my mother to take him back. He said that she listened only to me, and that I needed to do this for the family.

"I never told my mother to take him back, but they ended up staying together. I never had much of a relationship with my father. I never really saw my parents as 'parents.' I was happy to see my sister have the relationship I didn't have with my father, but I never really wanted that for myself. I suppose it was a defense mechanism to keep myself from being hurt."

Ivonne's home life took a turn for the worse...and then God dramatically intervened.

When Hope Arrived

"Few people get to see the exact moment in their life when God intervenes and changes it forever," Ivonne said. "I had that opportunity in junior high."

One day as Ivonne picked up her siblings from their elementary school, they caused some "trouble" and were reported to Ivonne's junior high school vice principal and counselor, Miss Perini.

Miss Perini insisted that Ivonne start volunteering her time in the school office after she got out of school as a way of "serving time" for the trouble she had been in.

"Miss Perini had many children come and go in her life, but little did she know at the time that God had other plans for her...and for me," Ivonne said.

"After I served my time in the office I would come in on my own time and volunteer to help, simply because Miss Perini would trust me with work. She also listened as I shared about my problems at home, and she made sure I was doing well in school. Even after I moved on to ninth grade, I still came back in the afternoons to help out at the junior high office. I felt validated and safe there. Unbeknownst to me, Miss Perini would meet with my teachers to make sure I was doing all right in school.

"It was during ninth grade that I saw a movie in which a man forced himself on a girl, and all my repressed memories of my sexual abuse came flooding back. For years I had repressed my experience, and suddenly it was right there in front of me. I had a hard time dealing with that. Between my problems at home, dealing with my repressed memories, and trying to function at school, I felt like I was going crazy.

"My sophomore year, things got so bad at home that I decided to run away. I went to Miss Perini to thank her for all her help, and then I left. I didn't have a plan. I just got on a bus and rode it all afternoon and all night. All the while I kept thinking, *I'm meant for more than this...this is not how my life is supposed to go.* So I got off the bus and returned home. I finally told my family and Miss Perini about my repressed memories and all the stresses of home, but my parents simply denied anything had happened and went back to the status quo.

Miss Perini tried to counsel my family, but my parents were very prideful and wouldn't listen or admit there was a problem.

"Later on, I ran away again—only this time to Miss Perini's house. From that night on, I never went back home. I eventually became Miss Perini's legally adopted daughter. I have often thanked her for letting God use her to save my life, but she always replies, 'I've known many children in my life, but you were meant to save *my life.*'

"From that moment forward I knew what *I was meant for more than this* looked like in my life. I was meant to be Christ's child. And an encouraging, hopeful confidence that there was more to my life than the pain or disappointment was revealed on October 28, 1990, when I surrendered my life to Jesus Christ and became a part of *His* family. What's interesting is that I had always felt God's presence in my life. But I hadn't known what it meant to surrender my life to Him and become His child."

Another Heartache

When Ivonne turned her life over to Christ, her heartaches didn't suddenly go away.

"I wish I could say it was all joy after that, but it wasn't. I went through some depressing years during which I was separated from my siblings and felt like I had betrayed my parents. Although they were part of the reason I had left home, I felt unworthy of my mom's love and care.

"After many years of healing, I realized all that had happened to me was for God's purpose, and I wanted to give something back to those who had gone through similar experiences. So I set aside my aspirations to become an actress and became a teacher, a high school counselor at my church, and a mentor at a city high school program."

While all that was taking place, Ivonne fell in love for the first time. She met a man at a restaurant where she worked during the summers. Although he lived out of town, she went home and told Miss Perini (who was her mother by this time) that although she believed she'd never see him again, she had met her "husband." They both laughed at that.

Three months later this man walked into one of the high school ministry meetings at the church Ivonne attended. He had moved to town and started attending her church.

They dated off and on for four years, and Ivonne said, "All along I felt that something was not right, but I knew I was too weak to break up with him. Full of fear, I got on my knees one evening and asked Jesus, 'If this man and I are not meant to be together, then please have *him* break up with me.'"

Exactly one week later this man broke up with Ivonne, telling her he didn't feel the way he thought he would feel toward her.

Ivonne was crushed, but then realized that God had answered her prayer. "Jesus had prepared my heart by bringing me to my knees and causing me to pray about it in the first place."

Ivonne saw the man a year later, at which time he admitted to her that he had walked away from the church and was living a homosexual lifestyle.

"We met a week later and he told me all about his experiences and struggles. He told me he wanted to remain friends and that even though he wasn't in love with me, he loved me more than any woman he had ever loved. In summary, he pretty much told me everything I ever wanted to hear. But I knew any kind of relationship had nowhere to go because he was living a homosexual lifestyle."

After that conversation, Ivonne became more convinced than ever that God knew what He was doing when He had allowed their breakup a year earlier. She tried to remain the man's friend, at his request, but it broke her heart to continually hear of his relationships with other men. So she ended contact with him.

"I was confronted with a great deal of trust issues again, but this time I was left with not trusting myself. How could I be with someone for that long and not see this coming? Could it be that I wanted something so much that I couldn't see the truth?

"I trusted God and felt confident I would get through the pain, but oddly I didn't trust my ability to judge the character of men. For a long time I didn't date, and often I would say I was ready to give my heart away again, but I never did. For years I was afraid of being hurt again."

Ivonne realizes now that Jesus was restoring in her a new sense of worth—a sense that had been shattered by the broken relationship she had experienced earlier.

Realizing There's a Reason

Today, at 40 years old, Ivonne says, "I wanted to be married with children…I'm not.

"I wanted to buy a home with my husband…I bought a house all by myself two years ago.

"I wanted to come home to my husband and share my day…I come home to my dog, a dinner with friends, or a call to a family member.

"I wanted someone to go to the beach with…I go alone, with my Bible and a good book."

Although life has turned out very different than the way Ivonne or others think it should have, she maintains hope that the God who had something more for her isn't done with her yet.

"Although many of my life experiences did not make sense at the time they happened, God has always taught me that they have happened for a reason," she says.

Part of that reason, she says, is that she knows who she is in the eyes of her Creator.

"I am not Ivonne the immigrant child, Ivonne the sexually abused victim, Ivonne the product of a marital affair, Ivonne who almost married a gay man, Ivonne who has to do things on her own. I am—and continue to be—Ivonne the woman whom God is shaping into what *He* wants for His kingdom!

"I am a firm believer that all in my life has happened for a divine purpose, and that purpose is so that I can be used by God," she says.

Ivonne admits she is still lonely at times.

"I want more than ever to share my life with a man, I want to find my best friend and grow old with him, but I am learning that loneliness is a part of life whether a person is married or single. I'm learning that this part of my journey is preparing me for God's next purpose in my life."

Ivonne said she is not temped to settle for just anyone at this point. "I deserve more than 'just anybody.' I remember that at a young age

God told me I was *meant for more than this,* and that includes my relationship with men. How can I have been brought through all that God has brought me through and not believe that He wants the best for me?

"I don't know if I'll ever get married, and even saying that scares me because I do want to be married. But I have never done things because they were 'the next thing to do.' I could have married one of the many whom I've met and dated. I could have had a child because society says I should have one by now. I could have slept around simply because I had opportunities, and I could be tempted to stay in my depressed, hopeless state of mind at times because I don't have any of the above. But I *choose* to trust that God still has a purpose and a plan for me.

"I'm learning that life is greater than just waiting for the next thing to come, including a husband and children. It's looking at life and making the most of what has *already* come."

Pondering the Purpose

Ivonne is not the only woman whose life has played out a certain way for a reason. She is not a special case, singled out by God because He happens to like her more than you or me. Ivonne is just one example of a woman who *chooses* to see God's hand and His purposes in her life. She *chooses* to trust that He is working everything in her life for good. And you can choose to be a woman who sees God at work in *your* life, too.

Step back with me for a moment and look at what was obviously God's providential hand at work in Ivonne's life:

Her Pain	God's Purpose
She suffered through a painful childhood	She now has a heart for children and their suffering
She had nowhere to go and a mentor took her in	She now mentors young girls who have nowhere to go
She was the victim of sexual assault	She now counsels other sexual assault victims
She couldn't marry the man she wanted	She now knows to wait on *God's* best for her

Do you see the intricately woven pattern of God's sovereign, all-knowing goodness in Ivonne's life? Where she might have seen God's punishment, she instead sees God's provision. What she could have seen as reasons to be bitter she today sees as blessings. That's being able to find purpose in your pain.

We sometimes look at painful circumstances and conclude that our lives are out of control. Yet that may be precisely when God is *taking* control and engineering our circumstances for the better.

The Bible says in Romans 8:28-29:

> We know that all things work together for good to those who love God, to those who are the called according to His purpose. For whom He foreknew, He also predestined to be conformed to the image of His Son.

That passage tells us two things about God's purposes and plans for our lives:

1. God has the ability to take *all* things—even the hurtful things, even the things we didn't plan on or expect—and turn them into something truly good in our lives.

2. God's intention is to make us more like His Son, Jesus, so that we think, speak, and act like Him. That means God desires to use whatever has happened in your life—whatever has hurt you—to make you more like His Son. Are you willing to be molded and shaped so that you become more like Christ?

In his beloved classic, *My Utmost for His Highest*, Oswald Chambers wrote:

> As we grow in the Christian life, it becomes simpler to us, because we are less inclined to say, "I wonder why God allowed this or that?" And we begin to see that the compelling purpose of God lies behind everything in life, and that God is divinely shaping us into oneness with that purpose.[1]

In Jeremiah 18:1-6, we gain more insight about who we are in the hands of our all-sovereign God. In this passage God tells His prophet, Jeremiah, to watch a potter at his wheel and learn a lesson about God's authority to shape His people as He chooses:

> The LORD gave another message to Jeremiah. He said, "Go down to the shop where clay pots and jars are made. I will speak to you while you are there." So I did as he told me and found the potter working at his wheel. But the jar he was making did not turn out as he had hoped, so the potter squashed the jar into a lump of clay and started again. Then the Lord gave me this message: "O Israel, can I not do to you as this potter has done to his clay? As the clay is in the potter's hand, so are you in my hand" (NLT).

God was basically saying, "In the same way that the potter has absolute authority over the way he decides to fashion the clay, so the Lord God has the power to do what He chooses with His people."

Does God have a right to do with you and me as He pleases? Yes. Even if it means interfering with our plans? Absolutely. Even if it means allowing some pain into our lives because of how that pain will shape us and grow us? Apparently so. But the good news is this: God's ways are perfect. He never makes mistakes.[2]

We see a beautiful example of the way God's purposes can turn out for the best in the Old Testament account about Joseph. If you were to ask Joseph what life was like for him while he was growing up, he could say, "I grew up in a terribly dysfunctional family. In fact, all my brothers hated me. Because of their hatred, I was sold into slavery. Then later I was falsely accused of doing wrong, and imprisoned for more than two years. My life was a real mess!"

Yet Joseph never described his life that way. He never pointed fingers at his brothers or started in with the "Where was God?" complaint. Instead, from a palace throne, Joseph summarized his life by recognizing God's providence and goodness. What you and I might consider a mess was a masterpiece. God had worked through negative circumstances and divinely orchestrated His purposes not only for Joseph's life, but also for the lives of an entire race of people.

Joseph's Journey

Like Ivonne, Joseph knew early on that God had plans for him. He had ten older brothers, and Joseph ended up being the favored son of their father, Jacob. This caused the brothers to be jealous and to hate Joseph. Their father had made a brightly colored coat for Joseph and hadn't made one for any of them, and Jacob doted on Joseph like he was the cat's meow. And the hatred and envy only escalated when Joseph told his brothers one day of a prophetic dream he had—a dream in which his brothers (and even his parents) bowed down to him. (Can you imagine the nerve he had telling his ten older brothers about this dream?)

Apparently for Joseph's brothers, this dream was the last straw. They schemed to be rid of him once and for all. On a journey far from home, they threw Joseph into a pit, sold him into slavery, and then fabricated a story to their father about Joseph's disappearance. They dipped Joseph's brightly colored coat into goat blood and showed the coat to Jacob, leading him to conclude that his favorite son had been killed by a wild animal.

With the exception of Jacob, who believed Joseph was dead, no one even missed Joseph after he was sold into slavery and ended up in Egypt. But God was with him. Joseph became favored by a man named Potiphar, who was an officer of Pharaoh. When Potiphar saw how Joseph excelled at all that he did, he placed Joseph in charge of all that he owned. Joseph governed this man's estate efficiently and with integrity, and the Lord blessed all that he did.

In the meantime, Potiphar's wife, who was deeply attracted to Joseph, made repeated sexual advances to him. Joseph persistently declined, and eventually told her that he could never sleep with her— out of loyalty to his master and to his God. Out of anger, Potiphar's wife framed Joseph and had him arrested for assaulting *her*! Joseph ended up being thrown into prison for simply doing the *right* thing. Talk about getting a bad break!

While Joseph was in prison, he ended up interpreting the dreams of a cupbearer and a baker. Both men had formerly served the Pharaoh but had been arrested and thrown into prison. The cupbearer had promised Joseph that when he got out, he'd put in a good word for him because of his ability to interpret dreams. But after the cupbearer was released, he forgot all about his promise.

Joseph remained in prison another two years. Then the Pharaoh had a dream, and none of the magicians and wise men of Egypt could interpret it. The cupbearer then remembered Joseph, and told the Pharaoh about his ability to interpret dreams. The Pharaoh called upon Joseph and was so pleased when Joseph interpreted his dream that he promoted Joseph to second-in-command in all of Egypt. Ultimately, it was because of Joseph's supervision of the grain supply in Egypt and his position of authority as governor that enabled him to spare the lives of his father, his brothers and their families, and many others who would've otherwise died of starvation back in Canaan.

Now, none of that would have been possible if Joseph hadn't been sold into slavery and hadn't been put into prison. Joseph endured years of injustice and real, physical pain, not to mention the inevitable emotional stress resulting from his unfair imprisonment. Yet behind the scenes, God was working a tremendous plan that would place Joseph in far better shoes than if he had never left his homeland.

And Joseph's legacy—in addition to sparing the lives of thousands in the land—was summed up in a statement he made to his brothers years later when he met them again face-to-face: "As for you, you meant evil against me; but God meant it for good" (Genesis 50:20). Instead of resenting their actions toward him, he recognized that his brothers' foolish actions, motivated by jealousy and rage, were used by God to turn his world around and serve a much bigger purpose. He recognized his life was not about his pleasure, but God's plan.[3] (We'll return to this story in chapter 8 when we look, in detail, at Joseph's heart of forgiveness toward those who had wronged him.)

Whether someone directly caused your pain or you experienced it indirectly, God can still use *your* pain for good, too. Is it possible that He is shaping your character in the midst of your pain and preparing to raise you up to a greater purpose as well?

Struggling to Understand

Sometimes we struggle with believing there's a greater purpose that will result from our pain because we can't see that purpose or imagine what it might be. But our inability to see or imagine what God has in mind doesn't mean He is not at work in our situation.

Joseph couldn't see any hope from a prison cell. He couldn't see himself as necessarily significant while working as a slave. But God saw Joseph's faithfulness in every situation he was in, and as Joseph waited upon God and trusted Him, his reward eventually came.

My friend Christi couldn't see the "good" in her husband's unfaithfulness to her just two years into their marriage. She had married the man she thought God wanted for her (although now she looks back and recognizes some of the warning signs early on that she failed to act upon). She had hoped to have children with him and live a happy life. Instead she found herself divorced, childless, and not liking where she was in life. For a couple years, she only saw the pain she was experiencing as a result of her ex-husband's sin. But eventually, as God worked in Christi's heart and filled her with a satisfaction in Him alone, He made her a mother of two beautiful adopted daughters—daughters she never would've known had her original marriage stayed intact.

Now, God didn't *cause* Christi's husband to be unfaithful, but He worked in spite of it for Christi's benefit. She will tell you today, in an instant, that her life is full and complete in Christ and His blessings. And the once-painful memories of her unfaithful husband are now part of a long-forgotten past.

In Psalm 30:5 we're told that "weeping may last through the night, but joy comes with the morning" (NLT). If you are still in what seems like a long, dark night, joy *will* come just as surely as the morning. In that Scripture verse, God was promising us that joy, like the morning, is inevitable when you give your sorrow to Him.

I, too, struggled to understand a difficulty God allowed in my life. I couldn't understand how my parents' divorce—when I was 19 years old—could possibly work for good in my life or anyone else's. Because I was raised in the church and my parents were both believers and in ministry, I never imagined my family would be torn apart through the effects of alcoholism and years of unresolved issues. One summer morning at a Christian camp where I was volunteering for a week as a high school camp counselor, I sat atop a huge rock and argued the point with God until He spoke clearly to me through His Word:

> "For My thoughts are not your thoughts
> Nor are your ways My ways," says the LORD.
> "For as the heavens are higher than the earth,
> So are My ways higher than your ways,
> And My thoughts than your thoughts" (Isaiah 55:8-9).

Never before had God's Word spoken so clearly to the depths of my heart. I was refusing to believe something because I couldn't understand it. And God was reinforcing to me, through those verses in Isaiah, that just because I didn't understand what was happening did not make Him any less able to work *all* things for good in my life.

God was basically saying, "I have My reasons for allowing this. And it is not essential that you understand. It is only essential that you *trust Me.*"

Today, it's been nearly 30 years since my parents' divorce. While I still don't understand it, I can honestly tell you that God has truly worked through it for good in all of our lives—including that of my father, who immediately entered an alcoholic recovery program and, in addition to remaining sober for nearly 30 years, has an effective ministry to recovering alcoholics. That day atop the rock was also a pivotal point in my life as I learned to surrender to God what I didn't understand. That lesson has carried me through many experiences in life since then. God didn't *cause* my parents' divorce—just like He didn't *cause* the hurts in *your* life. But He was able to work through it for good in my life and the lives of my other family members.

What About You?

What wounds in your life are you struggling to understand? A painful childhood? A hurtful breakup? A spouse's affair? The inability to conceive a child? The loss of a friend or a job? The onset of a disease or disability? It is not essential that you understand *why* you are hurting.

It *is* essential, however, that you *trust* the One who, in love, is allowing the hurt to happen. As you trust His goodness, His love, and His overall purpose in allowing what is happening in your life, you can grow and develop into the woman He is shaping you to be.

It is through our struggles that we are strengthened, through our pain that we are polished, and through our difficulties that we can discover a deeper intimacy with God. That, right there, is the good that God can work through our hurts in life. And sometimes we can't see those benefits right away. Strength and a deeper intimacy with God are characteristics that we sometimes don't see at all. But others will. And sometimes it's when others around us see the benefits of our pain that we can finally look back and say, "Aha—God *did* know what He was doing after all."

Will you trust that whatever God has allowed to happen in your life thus far is contributing to an overall purpose and design He has to mold you into the image of Christ?

As one writer has said:

> Sin, sorrow, and suffering *are,* and it is not for us to say that God has made a mistake in allowing them.
>
> Sorrow removes a great deal of a person's shallowness, but it does not always make that person better. Suffering either gives me to myself or it destroys me. You cannot find or receive yourself through success, because you lose your head over pride. And you cannot receive yourself through the monotony of your daily life, because you give in to complaining. The only way to find yourself is in the fires of sorrow. Why it should be this way is immaterial. The fact is that it is true in the Scriptures and in human experience.[4]

When you feel pain in your life, it's not because you're insignificant and God hasn't noticed you. No, my friend, quite the contrary is true. Rather, He has great plans for what He wants to do through you.

I wish I could say that my struggles with what God has allowed in my life were limited to that experience atop a rock when I was 19 years old. But I have struggled many times throughout my life with what

I believe would've been better for me than what God has ultimately allowed. Just recently I went through this again. I was focusing on something that wasn't going my way, and I found myself saying, "God, I would give up this ministry and everything I do today to just have this *one thing* I've always wanted."

Even as I spoke the words, I realized how very selfish they were. God's sole intention for my life is not to make me happy. It's to make me holy. It's not even about my purpose or fulfillment. It's about His glory. God desires that I be fully dependent on Him, and that I realize I am nothing in and of myself. And He knows the only way that will happen is if I continue to be dependent on Him for the *one thing* I was praying about. God has purposes that are much higher than mine. And honestly, as I look back on that foolish prayer, I am so grateful that He does.

That lesson I learned atop a rock nearly 30 years ago came back to my mind as if God were reiterating again Isaiah 55:8: "Cindi, if through a little pain in your life I can bring about a greater understanding in you of who I am and then cause you to share it with countless others, wouldn't that make it seem worthwhile? Do you exist for your own fulfillment, or to carry out My purposes? *For My ways are higher than your ways and My thoughts than your thoughts.*"

I was humbled to realize God can accomplish far more with a small amount of my pain than I can accomplish with a lifetime full of pleasure.

Giving It Up

It really isn't about me—or you. It's about what the Sovereign God of this Universe decides He wants to do with one woman who says to Him, "Not my will, but Yours. Not my comfort, but Your cause. Not my greed, but Your goodness. Not my desires, but Your delight."

Can you be a woman who says those words, even in the midst of the pain that may still persist in your heart? Can you say to Him, "Not my plan, but Yours, even if it hurts"?

Maybe you're thinking, *No, Cindi, I don't think I can say that right now. The pain is too deep and I just want it to stop.* If that's the case, my friend, Jesus understands. Because He, too, knows what it's like to experience deep suffering and pain.

Just before His arrest and execution, Jesus wrestled in prayer with His Father, saying, "My Father! *If it is possible, let this cup of suffering be taken away from me.* Yet I want your will, not mine." A second time, Jesus prayed, "My Father! If this cup cannot be taken away until I drink it, your will be done" (Matthew 26:39,42 NLT, emphasis added). Jesus was saying, "Father, if there's *any other way* to deliver people from sin, don't make Me go through with this." Yet He followed up that very human request with a godly act of obedience and surrender: "Yet not My will, but Yours."

Jesus was asking that if it were possible, God spare Him His death on the cross. Yet He also knew His impending death was God's provision for the reconciliation of the sins of mankind. He knew His surrender to the will of His Father would result in the forgiveness of sins for every person who would put their faith and trust in Jesus Christ for their salvation. Jesus ultimately wanted to please His Father, not save His own skin.

That is the part that really convicted my heart. In the times that I have tried to avoid pain or the loss of something, my life has not been at stake. Yet Jesus was faced with death when He prayed, "Not My will, but Yours." Jesus realized His suffering and death would bring about reconciliation between God and mankind. He realized that eternity, literally, was at stake.

And yet when I have prayed, "God, please spare me of this," who am I to think eternity is not at stake? The eternity of someone may very well be at stake when you or I want to avoid pain that God intends to use in our lives to touch, heal, comfort, or minister to someone else.

Yes, how often I want to save my own tears, my own discomfort, my own pride or embarrassment rather than let it all go so God and His purposes can proceed.

God can very well proceed in His purposes without us...but He wants us to willingly surrender to Him so that we can take part in what He wants to accomplish in and through us. Here's how to be a willing participant in the plans and purposes He has for your life:

1. Thank God in the Midst of Your Circumstances

First Thessalonians 5:18 says, "Give thanks in all circumstances; for this is God's will for you in Christ Jesus" (NIV). God's will—His purpose for you—is that you be thankful in *all* things...even the things which still hurt. To be able to say, "Thank You, God, even though I don't understand this" is an act of obedience and an exercise of faith. And there is no greater way to please God than through your obedience and faith.[5] Can you practice this huge step of surrender right now and thank Him for each painful moment you've been through not because you *feel* thankful, but because you are commanded to be thankful?

2. Tell God You're Ready to Grow

It is a mature believer who immediately recognizes that difficult and hurtful times are an opportunity to grow closer to God and learn the lessons He desires that we take to heart. By telling Him you're ready to grow, you are putting yourself in a position to be teachable, and opening your heart to what He has for you to learn. Not every hurtful situation in your life is because God wants to *teach* you something, but He can definitely *work through* every hurtful situation so that it doesn't end up being for nothing. Look for the lesson, if there is one, so you don't miss it. And keep a soft heart that is moldable to His touch.

3. Trust the Process

This is a phrase my pastor-husband has said to me since the early years of our marriage. And I've often heard him repeat it to others. Joseph apparently trusted the process when he let God use him in every situation he was in, no matter how painful. After he was sold as a slave to Potiphar, he worked hard and earned the man's respect and was given charge of his whole household, which he managed well. Then, when he was sent to prison after being falsely accused, he earned the prison guard's trust and was given authority to supervise all the other prisoners (Genesis 39:1-6,19-23). Joseph probably had no idea that God was preparing him to rule over all Egypt by first training him to rule over a man's household and servants, and then over an entire prison. Even if you can't see anything good coming out of your situation right now, trust the process God is allowing you to go through, which will prepare you for something greater later.

Our Simple Offering

Just as Ivonne continues to believe she was made for something more, you can believe it, too. Perhaps your life has not turned out the way you wanted, but it has gone exactly the way your heavenly Father knew it would, and He is still waiting for you to surrender your will and your wounds to Him and say, "I'm all Yours." By saying, "Not my will, but Yours," you are acknowledging that God is in control and that you are in His hands. And although it may not feel like it just now, there is no better place for you to be.

STEP #1 *Toward Healing and Wholeness*

Realize there's a reason—and a purpose—behind your pain.
And God's purposes are so much bigger and better than your own.

LET THE HEALING BEGIN

Here is where you will decide if you will just read words or allow God to heal your heart by taking the time to work through the questions and exercises at the end of each chapter. I know there is a heart in you waiting to be healed. So let the healing begin.

1. Try putting together a chart like the one I did on page 21, which looked at the pain and God's possible purposes in Ivonne's life. On the left side, list the wounds you still carry. On the right side, write a brief prayer acknowledging that God knows about it and asking Him to use it for good in your life. In chapter 10, I will have you revisit a chart like this and fill in what you believe God may be leading you toward in terms of a purpose from that area of pain. But for now, just thank Him for it. I've gone ahead and done the first entry so you can see what this would look like.

Pain	Praise
My parents' divorce when I was 19 years old	Thank You that You were there and that it didn't take You by surprise. Thank You that I drew closer to You during that time and learned to depend on You more than my parents or circumstances. Thank You that You used that as a defining—and growing—point in my relationship with You.

Now you try it:

Your Pain	Your Offering of Praise

2. Look up the following verses and next to each reference, write a prayerful response to the One who knows all about your life and is working in and through it even now.

Jeremiah 29:11—

Romans 8:28-29—

2 Corinthians 4:17-18—

3. The Bible lists in Galatians 5:22-23 the characteristics (or "fruit") of one who is controlled by the Spirit of God rather than their pain. List these characteristics below and circle the ones you have developed—or are developing now—through the pain you've endured. You might also want to add a few words about how that characteristic is playing out in your life as a reaffirmation that you are developing that character quality.

4. Look at the characteristics you checked above. Now look at Romans 8:28-29 again, noting particularly verse 29. Write a prayer of thanks below in response to what you wrote above and how God might *already* be working through your wounds for good and molding you into the image of His Son.

A Prayer of Surrender

Lord God, I bring You my brokenness and lay it at Your feet. This is not what I expected or wanted in my life, but I realize it's not my life to control and direct. You are the Potter and I am a lump of marred and wounded clay. You have Your reasons and Your design and purposes in mind. Although I don't understand what those reasons are, I trust that You do and that You will work this wound into something wonderful in my life. I don't yet understand the purpose that can come from this pain, but I know You are a God who will do as You please, and it pleases You to make me more like Your Son. I will trust the process. And I will trust You.

2

Why Did I Have to Hurt Like This?

Reshaping Your Understanding of God

S haron's eyes sparkle as she talks of the sweet fellowship she knows today with God. But one would never guess from her smile and serenity the scars that covered her heart for years.

From as far back as she can remember, Sharon felt unloved, unwanted, and used. A victim of child abuse and incest, she was told that bad things happened to children who were "evil." She possesses no baby pictures, experienced no bonding moments with her mother, and can recall no happy memories while growing up. For years all she knew were terror and shame, which stalked and haunted her into her adult years.

When Sharon was just a year old, her mother tried to kill both Sharon and herself by gassing them in their home. Her mother was then institutionalized and never released. Sharon was placed in the foster-care system for the first six years of her life and grew up believing she made people "sick" or crazy.

Instead of providing a refuge for her, the foster homes only brought more suffering. "I was duct-taped to chairs, had knives put to my throat, even a gun to my head," Sharon recalls. At the age of six, she witnessed a murder in the home where she was staying and was told, at gunpoint, to never speak about it or she'd be as dead as the man she saw lying on the floor.

Sharon stuffed the horrific incident inside herself and tried to move on.

When Sharon was seven she began living with her father, a sick and controlling man who was addicted to drugs. He physically and sexually abused her. Sharon struggled between wanting her father's love and not wanting him to hurt her. When she let him close to her physically, she thought he was expressing affection for her. But afterward he would resent her and treat her cruelly. So she was constantly hurt and confused.

When Sharon was 15 years old, her father got colon cancer and the sexual abuse stopped. Within four years he was dead. Her manipulative father had told her, shortly before dying, that she needed to kill herself when he died because no one would ever want her or love her.

Two years after her father died, Sharon married the first man who told her he "loved" her and repeated the dysfunctional patterns she learned growing up. "He told me once that he loved me, and I believed him," she said.

But Sharon had no idea what love was. All she had known was what she had interpreted as "love" from a distant father.

Sharon had two children with her husband and endured 20 years of a tumultuous relationship. Then, at 35 years old, she became extremely ill. It took doctors four years to determine that she had a very rare form of cancer that, upon diagnosing, was too late to treat. Upon hearing that death was imminent, Sharon was actually relieved. "I believed I'd die and I remember thinking, *Great, I can finally leave here and be rid of the pain.*" But the cancer didn't take her life. She remembers thinking at the time that all people go to heaven when they die, but because she was so "bad"—as she'd been told all her life—she wasn't good enough for heaven, so she couldn't even die.

Shortly after her diagnosis, Sharon and her husband divorced. She became a single mom who had lost her health, her job, and her home. Then she started remembering all the horrible things that had happened to her during childhood. Diagnosed with post-traumatic stress disorder (PTSD)—on top of the cancer—her childhood abuse hit her "like shrapnel...it just dropped in."

Sharon experienced about seven years of PTSD while she tried to get back on her feet. Her daughters were teenagers by then. She would work from eight to five, then after work, if her kids were settled, she'd drive to a park, sit in her car, listen to Christian music, and just scream.

"During the day I could live in denial about all that I had gone through because I was busy. But at the end of the day it would all flood back in again."

In an attempt to process what had happened to her as a child, she began keeping a journal and recording the events, feelings, and prayers that she could remember. It was at that time that she went to the police department and told a police sergeant everything she remembered about the murder she witnessed as a child. She begged the investigator to tell her she was crazy and that the incident had never happened, but she was told she had answered questions as a credible witness. The case was filed as an unsolved mystery.

It was also at this time that Sharon had to correct her beliefs about God. She had always "believed" God existed, but it was a god of *her* understanding, not God as He really is. She believed He was cruel, manipulative, and controlling, like her father.

"I always knew God was there, but I didn't know *who* God was. In my head, the God I knew growing up was as ugly as my father, as ugly as the incest and the pain I endured. God somehow took on a human form, and that's the only human form I could relate to—an angry, abusive father.

"I had a love-hate relationship with God. I wanted Him to help me, but I saw Him as mean and cruel and looking down at me with His finger pointed at me. I had a lot of faith, but I also had a lot of anger. There was a disconnect between my belief in God and what God looked like on a daily basis."

Discovering the Truth About God

One day Sharon was so angry with the hurt that happened in her life and the thought that God was punishing her that she shredded up a Bible and handed it to a pastor in a bucket and told him, "This is what I think of your God!" She had assumed the god she believed to exist was the same God of the Scriptures.

By the grace of God, that pastor responded to Sharon with great kindness. He showed her examples throughout the Bible—in the Psalms, in the book of Job, and in the letters of the apostle Paul—of people who had suffered most of their lives yet maintained faith and trust in God. He also shared with her his personal story of holding onto Jesus through the dry and painful times in his own life. He explained that pain is a part of life because of the sin that exists in this world, but God is not the one to blame for it. He is, instead, the One we hold onto in spite of it.

Sharon responded by telling the pastor, "I have to walk out of here believing with all my soul that *your* God is the good one and mine is not real."

Sharon said the shift in her thinking—and in her way of living—came when she decided that day to believe that God was good. "So I started imagining what kind of God I wanted my girls to live with in heaven. I had to believe in a God so different from the one I believed Him to be."

Can you imagine Sharon's relief and joy as she came to realize, through the Bible, that all that she had originally imagined God to be—full of love, compassion, kindness, gentleness, goodness, and forgiveness—was actually true? As Sharon got into God's Word, she began to discover the truth about Him:

- He wasn't a god who considered her "bad" and hated her. He is, instead, the God who said in His Word, "*I have loved you* with an everlasting love" (Jeremiah 31:3).

- He wasn't a god who was pointing his finger at her and waiting to punish her. He is, instead, the God who said in His Word, "I know the thoughts that I think toward you... thoughts of *peace* and not of evil, to give you a *future* and a *hope*" (Jeremiah 29:11).

- He wasn't a god who desired that she be punished. He is, rather, the God who is "not willing that any should perish but that all should come to repentance" (2 Peter 3:9).

- He wasn't a god who wanted her to suffer for his own

selfish gain. He is, instead, the God who laid down His life to suffer *in her place* so she would not have to be separated from Him for eternity (Romans 5:8).

- And he wasn't a god who would withdraw his love from her if she did something he didn't like or if he was in a bad mood. He is, instead, the God who says nothing can ever separate us from His love. Death can't, and life can't. The angels can't and the demons can't. Our fears for today, our worries about tomorrow, and even the powers of hell can't keep God's love away (Romans 8:38 NLT).

Is it possible that, through *your* hurts and heartaches, you have perceived God as being very different than He actually is? Maybe you haven't done that intentionally. Perhaps, like Sharon, you just put a face on Him that resembles someone who has hurt you. Many women, like Sharon did, tend to believe that God is very much like their earthly father. Therefore, if they had a father who was angry, abusive, absent, disapproving, or just emotionally uninvolved, they tend to see God as the same way. But the only way we can let God heal our hearts of the hurt we've experienced is to understand and get to know Him as He *really* is. As Scripture *says* He is.

Discovering the Truth About Yourself

Sharon also learned from Scripture how God sees *her*. She learned, from God's Word, that as good and clean as she tried to be, she could never earn God's love for her. His love was a gift made possible through the death and resurrection of His Son, Jesus. It was through Jesus' death on the cross that the penalty for her sin was paid, and a place in heaven was purchased for her. She also learned that once she surrendered her life to Jesus Christ and put her hope in His death on the cross, she became His child. She was no longer the child of a sick, depraved man. She was, instead, a precious child of God (Romans 8:14-17). She learned, too, that when she put her trust in Christ for her salvation, she became a new person spiritually. She was "not the same anymore, for the old life is gone. A new life has begun!" (2 Corinthians 5:17 NLT).

Can you look to a God like that to heal *your* heart? Can you release some old baggage that might be weighing you down by trusting in the God of the Bible rather than the god of your upbringing, the god of your ignorance, or the god of your fears?

Sharon realized she had a choice to either believe the truth about God or continue believing the lies of her childhood. "We live in our own realities," she said. "It is my choice today what story I will tell myself. Every day it got a little easier for me to believe the good God was true and the bad god was a lie."

Once Sharon knew the truth of who God is, she realized she could trust Him to bring healing to her heart.

"I really believed I was damaged to the core and God could never use me. I didn't want to be this damaged woman anymore and this woman who had cancer and this woman who was divorced. It was time to heal." A large part of Sharon's healing process involved praying to the true God of the Scriptures and asking Him to heal her in every way, using Psalm 139 as a guide.

"My goal was for God to search me and strip out everything in me that was not good, that was damaged, that was wounded."

A Healing Prayer from Scripture

In Psalm 139, David wrote about how God intimately knows each of us. He knows where we go, what we think, and even where we're trying to hide. David then talked of how we were intricately woven together in our mother's wombs. Even before we were born God wrote out the number of our days, and has constantly monitored us since. Then, toward the end of his song, David prayed:

> Search me, O God, and know my heart;
> Try me, and know my anxieties;
> And see if there is any wicked way in me,
> And lead me in the way everlasting (verses 23-24).

When we look at the original Hebrew words used in that passage, we discover it talks about more than just a prayer that God would look at our heart and take out anything bad.

The Hebrew word for "search" in that passage means "to examine intently." The Hebrew word for "try" means "to test," as with metals, with the goal of refining and purifying. The Hebrew word for "wicked" as used in verse 24 is a variation of the word *idol* or even *pain* or *sorrow*. And the word *way* means literally "a road" or "a course of life" or "a mode of action." So, in looking at the original language in which that prayer was written, it encourages us to pray something like this:

> Intensely examine me, O God, and know my innermost thoughts, intentions, and understanding. Test my quality and endurance like you would test precious metal and know my thoughts. And see if there exists in me any painful, sorrowful, or idolatrous course of action and guide me in the course of my life continually (or toward eternity).

Sharon knew she needed this kind of intense examination and purification because of the resentments, bitterness, fear, shame, and other things that were still lurking in the corners of her heart that she wasn't even aware of. Because of gods (through the form of people, habits, addictions, or obsessions) that could come her way and take the place of the one true God in her life. Because of something hidden within her that could cause her to travel down a road not glorifying to God.

"There was something intrinsic within me that was attracting these types of individuals to me (her father and ex-husband) and placing me in damaging situations. My prayer to God was this: 'Show me what is in my heart—the damage, the anger, the resentment, the extent of my wounds. And clean me so that I attract the kind of people You want to be around me.'"

You and I need this kind of examination and cleansing, too. We sometimes have no idea of the extent of brokenness that still exists in our lives, the amount of pain we still hold onto, the resentments that still lurk in the corners of our hearts, or the degree of bitterness that still resides in us. If David the psalmist, who knew a close, intimate relationship with God, needed to pray this kind of prayer, then you and I also need to pray for God to examine us and lead us in the course of His will, not our own. And when we ask God specifically to investigate our hearts and bring complete cleansing to our inner lives, He will hear us and He will heal us.

Exhibiting Wholeness

Sharon is whole today because she sought the true God of the Scriptures and asked Him to apply to her the cleansing power of His Word. She didn't assume she was beyond repair. Nor did she assume she was well enough to function on her own. She wanted to be whole and complete in God's eyes. She wanted to be held up to His standard and pass the test.

"The reason I have a life today and I can breathe is because at every turn I asked God to make me well. If I couldn't get well, I couldn't touch anybody, I couldn't minister to anybody, I couldn't help anybody."

That was the plea of Sharon's heart—to have the opportunity to show others the compassion she never received. To hold and love a child in the way she was never held or loved. To instill hope in a struggling teenager because she never saw such hope while growing up. Today, this woman, in spite of all she's gone through, has done all of the things I've just mentioned. She spent six years as a lead teacher at a charter school for at-risk students. And today she is the founder of A Path to Life Wellness Center—a nonprofit organization that serves, supports, and encourages women who have triumphed over all forms of cancer. She envisions the center will eventually become a place where, once women have completed their treatment, they can continue to come for acupuncture, dance therapy, laughter therapy, organic coffee, and so on.[1]

I have had the opportunity to sit across the table from Sharon on a few occasions and I can honestly tell you that she radiates with joy. She shows great compassion. There is no trace of a frightened, abused girl in her. There is no residue of bitterness. There is only a beautiful, confident, loving woman. And there is serenity in her presence. She exhibits a peace and a calm that is evidence of her rest and trust in the Lord despite having walked through the valley of the shadow of death—numerous times. She projects a hope and a passion for life. That is God's transforming presence—God's *healing*—in her life.

"The shift in my life came when I asked God to change *me*," Sharon said. "I had no power to change myself. He has always honored me at every step when I focused on Him changing me—not my husband, not that other person in my past."

God did work those changes in Sharon's life. He changed her heart. He filled her with Himself. He healed her from the inside out.

Eight years ago, Sharon married Dave—a man who truly loves her. Two months after they married, doctors discovered in Sharon another round of cancer. But at that point she realized she was in the hands of a loving, good, and tender God who knew what He was doing in her life. She went through radiation treatment and a recommended five years of nuclear testing before she would be considered clear of the disease. Seven years have gone by since, and she is still cancer-free.

"For many years, there was never anything that even resembled a peacefulness in my life," Sharon said. "But that's changed. Today, there's no drama anymore. There's nothing in me that goes to a place of insignificance."

Not even Sharon's *second* round of cancer derailed her. You and I might have, at that point, said: "Really, God? Again? Give me a break!" But Sharon held on to the God who loved her.

"Like Paul, I have learned to be content in whatever circumstances I am in," Sharon said, quoting Philippians 4:11, in which the apostle Paul talked about his contentment in spite of his many sufferings in life. She added: "Today I am content with who I am. I used to wake up thinking, *If I weren't me, life would be okay.* But today I know that because God is at work in me, life will be exceptional."

Dealing with the Hurts

Chances are your wounds are not as intense as Sharon's. But I included her story here so that, in case you can identify with any of what she faced, you can know that you are not alone—at least one other woman has lived through the same hurts and now experiences peace, joy, and complete healing. And if you haven't faced anything like what Sharon endured, her story is here so you can say, "I thank God I never had to suffer through *that.* "

I also realize that if your wounds aren't as intense as Sharon's, it does not make them any less painful to you. So I want to encourage you, right now, to take some of the steps Sharon took to find what she ultimately found—perfect love from a good and caring God, peace and contentment from the pain and confusion, and the real transformation that comes from being willing to say, "God, I trust who You are and believe You will make me into the woman You want me to be."

This, my friend, is where the healing begins.

1. List What's Still Lingering Inside of You

Sharon says, "I spent my entire life blaming someone else for my pain. Then I made the decision to change myself." She began recording in journals the events that she remembered had caused her pain. She did this not in an attempt to understand her pain, but to get it out. As she "got it out by writing it out" onto paper, it was as if God was stripping the pain out of her heart at the same time and putting it somewhere else.

Today Sharon points to the journals that record some of the most horrific events of her life and says, "These don't own me. It was my story, but I don't live it anymore."

If you feel ready to do this, go out and buy a pretty journal. Splurge if you have to. This is a place where you will bare your heart. In your journal, take time, perhaps every morning, to sit and just write what God leads you to write—memories that still plague you, offenses that come to mind every now and then, what you'd like to forget but can't seem to. As you write all this out, tell God you want these hurts out of your heart as well as your mind. Release the power that they might have on you by recognizing that God's power is even stronger and can redeem your hurts into something good.

As you write remember Psalm 62:8, which says, "Pour out your heart before Him; God is a refuge for us." What you write—and how you write it—is safe.

2. Look to Scripture to Reshape Your Understanding of God

What have you believed about God that isn't true? Have you come to believe He is punishing you by allowing pain in your life? Do you see Him as a judge who waits for you to mess up? As someone who is aloof and doesn't really care? Or as someone who truly is intimately acquainted with all your ways and loves you beyond reason?

Are you willing to come to the Scriptures with an open mind to receive the truth of who God says He is? Are you willing to let the Word of God replace the lies so you can begin to live and operate in the truth?

If there is someone you want to get to know, you will go to that person and spend time with them. That is what is required to really get to know God. It won't happen as you merely sit through a sermon on a Sunday morning or rely completely on the insights and observations of others. Yes, it is important for you to receive good Bible teaching. But you must also take the responsibility to get to know God yourself through the personal study of His Word. In the application section below I will guide you through an exercise so you can begin to do this.

3. Let God Examine You and Show You what Needs to Go

Sharon says before she started writing things down, "everything in me was empty and God had to rebuild this woman." But, she said, "Those are the moments I cherished more than anything—those moments when I said, 'God, just work on me. I don't need a man in my life. I don't need certain blessings, I just need You to make me clean.'"

Looking back now, Sharon said, she was compelled to pray that way. "I just had to be right with God. Nothing else mattered. I just had to be right and pure before Him."

You can, like Sharon, use Psalm 139:23-24 to guide your prayers. Or, maybe your wound is something you feel *you* are responsible for. In that case, you may want to pray through Psalm 51, a prayer of confession that the same psalm writer, David, wrote after a season in which he committed adultery—and murder—and realized he needed to be right before God once again. (In chapter 4 we will talk more about hurts we may have brought upon ourselves.)

Whatever the case, at the end of this chapter, you'll have the opportunity to pray and ask that God would examine you.

Taking That Next Step

I applaud your courage, dear sister, for being willing to take that next step and move away from your pool of pain and into a life of blessing, a life in which God heals your wounds from the inside out. My heart is always touched when I think of the story in Scripture of a man who had lain by a pool as an invalid for 38 years! He had been in his wounded condition for so long that when Jesus came and asked him if he wanted to be whole, he didn't answer the question. He simply came up with excuses for why he was still in the same old place after so many years. But Jesus wouldn't allow him to live out his days nursing his wounds in that hopeless condition. Jesus told the man, "Take up your bed and walk." Scripture tells us what happened next: "Immediately the man was made well, took up his bed, and walked" (John 5:1-8). You will not be like that man, staying in your place of pain for years on end. That will not be your story, my friend, because today is the day that Jesus is saying to *you,* "Take up your bed and walk!"

Jesus is right here, waiting to take your hand and lead you out of that place of pain and into a new tomorrow filled with hope and healing. He is the Great Physician, and He is ready to help you.

> ## STEP #2 *Toward Healing and Wholeness*
> Reshape your understanding of God through the Scriptures.
> *The true God of the Scriptures may be very different than the god you have perceived in your pain.*

<hr>

LET THE HEALING CONTINUE

1. Begin your journal writing. You can do this on a computer if you prefer, but there's something very intimate and personal about writing out your thoughts, as if you were writing a letter to God or writing your story as a keepsake for others. Think about a

time that is good for you to sit down, collect your thoughts, and write. When do you plan to journal your thoughts and prayers?

My time to journal: _____

My place to get alone and journal: _____

Look forward to this time with God and ask Him to guide your words as you become transparent with Him and yourself.

2. In the space below, let's get real. In the left column, list the frustrations you've experienced from people and circumstances in your life. Then in the center column, list what you needed in that moment or situation. Finally, in the column on the right, list what you have learned about what God offers you from pages 40-41. (If your particular need wasn't addressed on those pages, you might try looking up key words in your Bible's concordance or do a key word search on www.biblegateway.com to find the verses in Scripture that speak to your hurt.) I had Sharon fill out the first one to give you an example of how to complete this chart.

The frustrations I've experienced:	What I needed:	What God offers me:
Not having a mother while growing up	A mother's gentleness	John 8:32—God made me aware that He is with me and that truth would set me free.

3. As further encouragement and for a deeper awareness of who God is, read the following verses and write a prayerful response based on what you have learned about God's character. (This might be an exercise you choose to write in your journal as well.)

Psalm 139:17-18:

Psalm 147:3:

Isaiah 43:2:

2 Corinthians 1:3-4:

A Prayer of Healing

God, investigate my life;
   get all the facts firsthand.
I'm an open book to you;
   even from a distance, you know what I'm thinking...
You know me inside and out,
   you know every bone in my body;
You know exactly how I was made, bit by bit,
   how I was sculpted from nothing into something.
Like an open book, you watched me grow from
   conception to birth;
   all the stages of my life were spread out before you,
The days of my life all prepared before I'd even
   lived one day...
Investigate my life, O God,
   find out everything about me;
Cross-examine and test me,
   get a clear picture of what I'm about;
See for yourself whether I've done anything wrong—
   then guide me on the road to eternal life
            (Psalm 139:1-2,15-17,23-24 MSG).

God, You know the intimate details of my life and therefore my hurts are not hidden from You. Help me to sense Your love in spite of the heartache I've endured. Help me to see You as You really are, not as my pain has perceived You. In Your Word, Jesus, You say, "You will know the truth and the truth will set you free" (John 8:32 NIV). Lord, I long to know You and the truth of who You are, trusting that You alone will set me free.

3

Where Was God, Anyway?

Rejecting the Lie that He Didn't Care

Have you ever looked back on an incident in your life and wondered, *Where was God, anyway? Didn't He care? Why didn't He come to my rescue? What kind of God would let me go through something like that?*

Yet a woman who is allowing God to heal her hurts will look back on her life, with all its wounds and heartaches, and see God's protection and provision rather than His punishment.

Christina is one of those women who praises God in spite of the pain she grew up with. Considered by others around her as one of life's throwaways from the time she was a young child, Christina saw more than most of us ever care to during her early years of life. But even in the midst of the junk she grew up with, she knows God saw her little heart and was preparing for her a life—and a ministry.

Christina was born in Las Vegas, Nevada, to a 16-year-old girl and her boyfriend. Her parents' relationship was "toxic," as she called it, full of drugs and verbal and physical abuse. Their relationship broke off when Christina was five and her brother, Jimmy, was three.

At that point her mother was a drug-addicted blackjack dealer who would disappear for weeks at a time. Christina remembers being forgotten at school and often having to stay with her grandmother when it was discovered that her mother was gone again. By the time Christina was eight, her mother met a Cuban political refugee named Oswald in a nightclub. Because of their mutual passion for drugs, the two formed a very volatile, carnal relationship that led to making, using, and selling every drug imaginable.

By the time Christina was eight years old, she began helping to make the drugs, too. At age nine, she knew how to make, cut, and package every conceivable drug, including angel dust, heroin, methamphetamines, crack, and cocaine.

Christina's family became a major drug supplier along the California-Nevada border in the early 1980s, running drugs along the I-15 corridor between Las Vegas and Los Angeles.

"One of my earliest memories is of the FBI kicking in the door and going through our house and asking where the drugs were," Christina said. "I remember the scope of the light on the guns looking in the dark for the drugs. I was nine and my brother was seven.

"I wouldn't tell them where the drugs were. I feared physical repercussion from my mother more than I feared the law. I wouldn't speak. I wouldn't say anything."

Finally, after much pressure and being told by her grandmother that it was okay to reveal where the drugs were, Christina pulled back the lining on a picture and the drugs were lined up there in the wall. Her brother, Jimmy, removed the felt on a speaker and drugs were hidden in there, too.

After Christina's mother and Oswald were arrested, her mother opted for rehab, faked it, and opened post office boxes in several states and started receiving welfare checks. They ended up living in Victorville, California, in a small apartment. Oswald followed them there. By then, Christina's mother was pregnant with her fifth child.

"We could never be consistent in school because of our mother's continual fear of being caught for her illegal drug trafficking. We moved to Oro Grande, Victorville, Hesperia, the Lakes, Lucerne Valley, Joshua Tree, Apple Valley, and finally, Helendale—in the Mojave Desert. There were others out there who were avoiding the law like we were. It was homestead land. And there was bestiality, plural marriage, polygamy, drug dealing, everything imaginable and unimaginable."

Christina remembers being in Helendale and trying to avoid the law and not having a home. "Oswald decided to build us a house, so he went to an auction in Lancaster and bought twenty-seven doors. We actually had a house made of twenty-seven doors, and an outhouse over a hole in the ground for a restroom."

There were no utilities, and no neighbors for at least a mile. They hauled in water. They were in a completely desolate area.

"About that time Jimmy and I started collecting railroad ties to build a fence to keep out coyotes and poisonous snakes around our house of twenty-seven doors," Christina said. "At our young age, we needed something for security, so we decided to build a fence around our house. We began to dig trenches and fill them with chicken wire and then we collected railroad ties."

When Hope Drove Up in a Bus

One morning while Christina and Jimmy were building their fence, she noticed a vehicle going from one living area to the next. In their part of the desert, all the roads were dirt, so every time the vehicle moved, Christina could see clouds of dust in the air. Since there usually were no visitors out where they lived, she wondered what was going on. She remembered thinking, *The propane guy came yesterday. Why is this vehicle moving from house to house?*

Eventually Christina saw that it was a bus, and it pulled up in front of their house. A man with a Southern drawl opened the door of the bus and said, "We're goin' to Vacation Bible School. Would you like to go?"

"I looked at Jimmy and he looked at me. I said, 'I don't know what it is,' and Jimmy said, 'I don't either, but there's other kids in there.' So we went in the house and asked our mother, 'Can we go to Vacation Bible School? There's a man out there picking up kids in a bus.' My mother answered, 'I don't care where the &*#@ you go, just get out of my #$&@ face!'"

It was a 45-minute ride to a tiny building called Oro Grande Community Church. "That man drove forty-five miles out of his way to pick up the worst of the worst in the most desolate and rejected place," Christina said.

"We weren't cute kids, mind you. We were dirty. We took baths in a five-gallon bucket. We didn't have matching, clean clothes. We were dirty, scrawny kids."

Christina remembers entering the little church and feeling her scars. "I had a scar on my chin from being thrown into a piano. Jimmy and I were physically scarred, emotionally scarred, and spiritually scarred.

"We walked in, sat in a pew, and I remember just smiling. I remember *seeing* peace. I wasn't used to seeing peace. I wasn't used to seeing people who wanted to see children.

"I remember seeing other kids who looked dirty just like us. And I remember that everyone smiled. And I saw *teeth*…" (extended drug use had worn away the teeth of nearly all the adults she knew).

"These people were actually happy to be around us kids," Christina said.

The pastor of the little church stood up and walked to the podium and spoke:

"He could've said anything that day, but he said, 'Do you need the *hope* of Jesus?' As I look back on that, I realize he could have said, 'Do you need the *love* of Jesus?' Or 'Do you need the *grace* of Jesus?' Or even 'Do you need the *life* of Jesus?'

"But he used the word *hope*.

"My middle name was Hope. And I knew I didn't have any.

"I remember thinking *I need hope,* because I understood, even at that age, that the lifestyle we were living was not normal. I understood we were avoiding the law. I understood we were taught to never speak to anyone about our life. I remember thinking information meant power, and you don't share information with anyone.

"I looked over at Jimmy and said, 'Jimmy, I need the hope of Jesus.' And he looked at me and said, 'Chrissy, I need the hope of Jesus, too.'"

Christina and Jimmy both prayed in that little church and surrendered their lives to Jesus, acknowledging that He died on the cross to redeem their lives and give them hope.

"I remember the smiles more than anything," Christina said. "And after we prayed to receive Jesus, the pastor talked about the persecuted church.

"Jimmy and I took our popsicle-stringed crosses and went back to our home in the dirt and I told my mother I received Jesus that day. She said, 'I don't care. What has Jesus ever done for us? Look where we're living.' She couldn't take responsibility for her actions or see that her life was a result of her sin. She then hit me and punched Jimmy. And Jimmy, having the sense of humor that he always had, said, 'See, Chrissy? We're already being the persecuted church!'"

By the time Christina was in sixth grade, her mother, pregnant with her sixth child, told Christina to drop out of school and take care of her brothers and sisters. She warned that if Christina didn't do that, they would all be turned over to Child Protective Services.

"So with that guilt hanging over my head, I dropped out of sixth grade to care for my siblings," Christina said.

As a sixth grader, Christina was taking care of the newborn baby, feeding him in the middle of the night, and doing everything her mother was incapable of doing because of her out-of-control, drug-addicted life.

Moving Out and Moving On

At 17 years old, Christina left home, fell in love with the man she's married to now, and went to college.

"For a while I lived not knowing what a Christian's life should look like. I was never discipled, never taught the Word of God. All I had done was say a prayer and receive Jesus. Yet I knew that my life should look different than it did. In college, I remember hearing God clearly speak to my heart: 'You're not giving all of yourself to Me. You're not experiencing victory because you don't really *know* Me.'"

That's when Christina became determined to do everything she could to get to know this God she had received in her heart when she was nine years old.

"I began taking a Bible study that would impact me forever. It was an inductive study, precept upon precept. Once I started studying the Bible verse by verse, looking to the Word for healing, for hope, for completeness, I prayed to the Lord and said, 'I am a broken, depraved mess. I hear my thoughts. I know what's on my hard drive. I need You to write a new one.'

"That's exactly what God did as I searched for Him and His heart and His will for my life, with the help of His Word. And as I absorbed more and more of His Word, I began noticing victories in my life. I began to experience the freedom that comes from obeying Scripture."

Christina is now in her mid-thirties. She and her husband of fifteen years have three biological children and have adopted a fourth child. And the only way you'd know that Christina was once in the pit is by hearing her testimony, which she boldly proclaims to give God the glory for redeeming her life. Today Christina Goleman is the director of women's ministries at her church, a Bible study teacher, a speaker for women's groups, and the director of a 200-member Vacation Bible School. She is full of passion for studying and teaching God's Word, full of life, and full of love for the God she is convinced was in control of all that she experienced as a child. She exhibits a confidence that she will instantly tell you is not *self*-confidence but God-confidence...confidence in the One who loved her and gave Himself for her. Confidence in the One who redeemed her life from the pit.

Although Christina experienced a tough childhood, she knows God was there, and she knows He heard the prayers of a nine-year-old girl and forever changed her heart. God knew what He was doing by allowing her to grow up in the miry depths so He could ultimately pull her up from the pit. And today she has a story to tell of the God who was absolutely sovereign over all that happened in her life.

God Saw Your Story

I have long found it a great comfort to know that God is absolutely sovereign over all things. That means nothing takes Him by surprise, and nothing happens outside of His control. Sometimes we don't like this truth because we have great difficulty trying to figure out why God didn't rescue us sooner or in some other way. Yet God knows what is best for us in the overall design of His purposes and His shaping of our character. He will allow us to endure what we think is bad in order to bring some good out of it in our lives and in the lives of others.

The Bible tells us there is nothing about us that God is not fully aware of. In Psalm 139—the same song in Scripture that Sharon lifted up to God for healing and transformation in her life—we learn of God's perfect and intimate knowledge of each of us. He has a constant, moment-by-moment awareness of all that is going on in our lives. If you've ever struggled with feeling unnoticed, forgotten, or insignificant, look with me at the tremendous value you carry in the eyes of your Creator. In this one psalm alone, we discover that God...

- *Intimately examines you,* not to find your faults but to know all about you[1] (verse 1).

- Knows where you hang out, what time you get up in the morning, and what you're thinking before the thought even comes your way. Not only are you noticed, you are constantly *watched over* (verse 2).

- Familiarizes Himself with your course of life or mode of action. He is not only familiar with your ways of doing things; He has them *memorized* (verse 3) .

- Knows what you're going to say before you say it (verse 4).

- Places hedges around you to keep you safe. In other words, God *hovers* over you[2] (verse 5).

- Won't let you wander out of His sight. He is aware of everywhere you go, run, or try to escape. You can't lose Him; He sticks to you like glue (verses 7-12).

Yes, God was there with you, alright. He has never let you *out* of His sight.

So Where Was the Rescue?

So if God constantly watches over us and has our ways memorized, why does He sometimes seem to stand by and allow hurts to run havoc in our lives? We looked at that question in the first chapter and discovered that God often has a purpose behind our pain and is shaping us into someone who can be a blessing in the lives of others. Now let me present another possible answer: What if God *did* rescue you in your situation but you didn't realize it? What if the pain you experienced was part of your deliverance from what could have been a deeper or more devastating pain?

Christina doesn't hold God responsible for what she grew up with. Rather, she looks back at certain situations and sees God's protection over her, rather than His negligence.

When Christina was a young teenager caring for her siblings, she recalls a strange man coming into their house one afternoon. She knew something wasn't right with him. She made eye contact with him and heard him ask her mother, "How much?" Immediately sensing danger, Christina rushed her brothers and sisters into a closet in the back of the house and told them, "We need to pray."

She started praying and pleading: "Please God, don't let this happen." She didn't know what was coming, but felt an overwhelming sense of dread as well as an urge to pray for God's protection over her family.

As Christina and her little brothers and sisters prayed and called out to the Lord for help, she sensed a peace and a confidence and, in childlike faith, she walked back into the room where her mother and the strange man were waiting. As soon as Christina made eye contact with the man, he bolted out of the house and never returned.

"I know now that greater is He who is in me than he who is in the world," she said, referring to 1 John 4:4. "I wasn't mature in my faith. No one had taught me the Word or discipled me since that prayer I uttered at Vacation Bible School. But I knew God's presence was with me and that I could cry out to Him for help."

After the man fled, Christina started to cry. The intensity of the moment had overwhelmed her. "I was confused. I was shaking. I didn't know exactly what had happened. I went back into the bedroom to check on my siblings, and they were all asleep—all five of them. And then I came back into the other room, and my mom and stepdad were asleep, too.

"It was as if God had put His hand over the entire home and hushed it—as if He had lulled everyone to sleep."

So many times we angrily look back on events in our life and ask, "Where was God? How could He have allowed that to happen? Doesn't

He care about me?" But Christina is one who looks back and knows God's hand of protection was over her.

"The bottom line is that God was in control," she said. Instead of pointing her finger at God and saying, "You could've prevented this!" she praises Him for protecting her from so much more that *could* have happened.

Pointing the Finger in Blame

Scripture records for us a story of two women who were very close to Jesus—and who may have felt like pointing their fingers at Him in blame when He didn't show up at a time when they really needed Him.

Martha and Mary were two sisters who had grown close to Jesus during His ministry on earth. They had hosted Him and His disciples in their home for dinner and were considered good friends of His (Luke 10:38-42). In fact, Scripture says, "Jesus loved Martha and her sister and Lazarus [their brother]" (John 11:5). So it must have come as a shock—or at least a grave disappointment—to these women when Jesus appeared to ignore their request, sent through a messenger, to come quickly to their town of Bethany because their brother, Lazarus, was dying.

In fact, Scripture tells us in John chapter 11 of Jesus' seemingly odd response:

> When Jesus heard that, He said, "This sickness is not unto death, but for the glory of God, that the Son of God may be glorified through it." Now Jesus loved Martha and her sister and Lazarus. So, when He heard that he was sick, He stayed *two more days* in the place where He was (verse 4, emphasis added).

Now, doesn't it seem strange that Jesus waited *two more days* before turning around and making the 20-mile trip on foot back to the village of Bethany to help Lazarus? After all, we are told He loved them. I'm sure that when Martha and Mary got word that their message was delivered but Jesus didn't come, they were quite disillusioned. *Doesn't He care? Doesn't He understand how bad this is? Doesn't He know that we wouldn't have bothered Him and told Him to come back this far if we didn't think it was serious? Jesus, how* **could** *You?*

When Jesus finally made the long journey back to Bethany, He told His followers, "Lazarus is dead, and for your sake I am glad I was not there, so that you may believe. But let us go to him" (verses 14-15 NIV).

By the time Jesus arrived, Lazarus had been dead for four days. *Four whole days.* Mary and Martha grieved for their brother, probably wondering all the while, *Where was Jesus? Why didn't He come? Why did He let this happen?* I can't imagine how much pain and disappointment they might have felt. After all, their Friend had the ability to heal their brother. Why hadn't He shown up while Lazarus was still alive?

As soon as Mary and Martha saw Jesus, they let Him know how hurt they were by His apparent lack of concern for their brother:

> Martha, as soon as she heard that Jesus was coming, went and met Him, but Mary was sitting in the house. Now Martha said to Jesus, "Lord, if You had been here, my brother would not have died. But even now I know that whatever You ask of God, God will give You."
>
> Jesus said to her, "Your brother will rise again."
>
> Martha said to Him, "I know that he will rise again in the resurrection at the last day."
>
> Jesus said to her, "I am the resurrection and the life. He who believes in Me, though he may die, he shall live. And whoever lives and believes in Me shall never die. Do you believe this?"
>
> She said to Him, "Yes, Lord, I believe that You are the Christ, the Son of God, who is to come into the world."
>
> And when she had said these things, she went her way and secretly called Mary her sister, saying, "The Teacher has come and is calling for you." As soon as she heard that, she arose quickly and came to Him (verses 20-27).

This gave Mary *her* chance to vent her frustration with Jesus as well:

"When Mary came where Jesus was, and saw Him, she fell down at His feet, saying to Him, 'Lord, if You had been here, my brother would not have died'" (verse 32).

At this point, Jesus could have rebuked these women for not trusting in the possibility He might have had a greater purpose behind allowing Lazarus to die. Because Jesus waited an extra two days before journeying back to Bethany, Lazarus had been in the tomb four whole days at the time of Jesus' arrival. In that time, anyone who was buried for four days was considered fully dead. This meant Jesus would do more than just heal a sick man—He would *raise him from the dead.* Jesus waited until the timing was perfect so He could perform this astounding miracle in front of all who came to mourn Lazarus's death.

Yes, Jesus could have eliminated four days of pain and suffering for two sisters if He had just healed their brother when they had requested Him to do so. But instead, Jesus waited so He could give the whole community—and eventually the entire world—an incredible testimony of His ability to bring the dead to life. He chose to not make a smaller rescue because He had a much greater one in mind.

Instead of healing Lazarus from a sickness—something He'd already done many times for people in that region—He was preparing to raise him from the dead!

When Mary and Martha made their request, they were thinking about the prospect of losing their brother. By contrast, Jesus was thinking of an entire world of people who would eventually hear about Him raising Lazarus from the dead. Through this hurtful situation that affected a small family, Jesus was getting ready to make one of His most powerful proclamations on earth: "I am the resurrection and the life. He who believes in Me, though he may die, he shall live. And whoever lives and believes in Me shall never die" (John 11:25-26).

Have you ever found yourself thinking, *How could You, God?* Have you ever wanted to argue with Him and say, "I needed You, but You didn't show up!" My friend, if God failed to act on a request for you a while ago, or still hasn't answered something you continue to ask of Him, it's safe to assume He has something greater in mind for you— or for the overall situation—than you do.

If Christina had known a different upbringing, she wouldn't have the powerful testimony she has today. If she hadn't become a Christian through a little Vacation Bible School program out in a remote area, she probably wouldn't be a Vacation Bible School director for more than 200 children today. And you wouldn't be reading of her story—and her faith in a God who knew what He was doing.

In chapter 1, I encouraged you to trust the process. Now I'm going to say the same thing in different words: Trust His silence.

His Silent Protection

When the terrorist attacks of September 11, 2001, hit the United States, my brother, Dan, worked at the FBI Headquarters in the J. Edgar Hoover Building in Washington, DC. He and his colleagues, from their workplace, heard the news coverage about the first plane crashing into the World Trade Center. Then they saw the live footage of the second plane hitting the twin towers. After getting word that the Pentagon had been hit, they immediately evacuated, as they guessed their building—and any other federal building—could be next.

Dan, a deacon in his church, was mindful of the fact that a large percentage of his church's congregation consisted of federal employees, and many of them worked at the Pentagon. He, the pastor, and the other deacons in the church started calling the families in the church that afternoon. By seven o'clock that evening, they had accounted for *every single one* of their members and attenders. Although many were working in the Pentagon at the time of the attack, thankfully, none of them had been in the part of the building that was hit. While many people across the nation that day may have been asking, "Where was God?" in the midst of the multiple tragedies, there was one church congregation that was praising God for His protection and provision down to the very last one of their own. So when disaster strikes, and we're inclined to focus on what's going wrong, we need to alert ourselves to the instances of God's provision and protection in the midst of that disaster.

God promised in His Word that He will never leave nor forsake us (Hebrews 13:5). In fact, no matter where we go, He is with us

(Psalm 139:7-11). That means He has been with you in everything you've faced. Maybe you just don't remember the sudden turn of events in which something worse could've happened, but didn't. Maybe you don't recall or even realize the rescues. The bottom line is, God cares about you. He knows what He is doing when He allows things to happen in your life. And He's with you right now as you read the pages of this book, ready to redeem your hurts and turn them into something greater than you have imagined.

Today, Christina keeps her focus on the God who provides and protects by maintaining a perspective of praise. Instead of harboring bitterness or resentment over what she experienced—or never experienced—as a child, she instead compares what she lacked to what she now has in her relationship with Christ.

"Even if my mom prepared nothing for me, Christ has been preparing a place for me for 2000 years [John 14:3]. Do I believe it? You better believe I do," she said with great confidence.

Even though there was a time when Christina had to search for food in dumpsters, God has promised to supply all her needs according to His riches in Christ Jesus (Philippians 4:19). Does she believe that? Oh, yes.

Even if Christina was rejected by her parents, God has promised He will never leave her nor forsake her (Hebrews 13:5). Does she bank on that so she is no longer insecure? Absolutely.

Pulled from the Pit

In Psalm 40, we read of the songwriter's praise to God for pulling him up out of the pit. It is a song that Joseph of the Old Testament could have sung. It is a song today that Christina surely sings. And it is a song you can sing, too, as you recognize that God sees your plight and can lift you from the pit:

> I waited patiently for the LORD;
> And He inclined to me,
> And heard my cry.
> He also brought me up out of a horrible pit,

> Out of the miry clay,
> And set my feet upon a rock,
> And established my steps.
> He has put a new song in my mouth—
> Praise to our God;
> Many will see it and fear,
> And will trust the LORD (verses 1-3).

Since you're reading this book right now, I'm guessing it's safe to say that you want to move forward from your pain. That is God working in you to accomplish His purposes. Allow God to set your feet upon a rock of understanding and trust that, as you do, He will put a new song in your mouth. And many will see the transformation God has made in you and come to trust the Lord themselves as a result.

Time to Trust

Can you, like David, rejoice that God has pulled you from the pit and set your feet upon a rock and given you a new song?

Can you, like Christina, see His protection rather than His punishment in spite of the hurts you have endured in your life? Can you trust that He wants to raise you up out of the pit as He did with David and Christina and as He will do with anyone who surrenders his or her life to Him? And can you trust Him with the proclamation He wants to make, through your pain, so that others can see that He is the resurrection and the life?

I know you can. And I'm right here with you as you take another courageous step toward the healing and wholeness God has for you.

STEP #3 *Toward Healing and Wholeness*

Reject the lie that God didn't care about the hurt you've experienced.

*God was there. He cares. And He is still working
His plan in your life.*

LET THE HEALING CONTINUE

1. Adopt the mindset Christina has to gain a new perspective on what God might've had in mind when He allowed you to experience what you did. Recall what you learned in this chapter from Psalm 139 if it helps. (I did the first couple for you.)

What I lacked:	What I now have in Christ:
Stability in my family; parents divorced when I was 19.	A new lineage in Him (Psalm 16).
I never felt "pretty" as a child.	I am fearfully and wonderfully made (Psalm 139:14).

2. Tell the Lord about a time when you were disappointed that He didn't seem to "show up." Confess that this made you feel unimportant to Him.

3. Now practice trust and surrender by thanking God, regardless of how you feel, for being with you as you experienced pain and for never letting you out of His sight. Write out your thank-you to God here so you can get the words out of your heart and onto paper.

4. Look up the following verses in your Bible and write each one out below. Circle the words that resonate with your heart, and next to each verse write a brief prayerful response.

   Psalm 4:8:

   Psalm 46:1-3:

   Psalm 121:2-3:

   Hebrews 13:5:

5. Choose one of the verses above and commit yourself to saying it aloud every morning this week so you can reinforce its truth in your mind. It's your first step toward renewing your mind to think of yourself as Christ does—as one who really matters to Him.

   The verse I will say aloud each morning is _____.

A Prayer from
Your Father's Heart to Yours

Beloved,
I have formed you in your mother's womb and am
intimately acquainted with all your ways. There is not a
thought in your mind, nor a word on your tongue, nor an
intention in your heart that I do not already know. There
is not a place where you can wander where you will be out-
side of My sight. Not a day in your life has occurred that I
have not allowed, and not a wound has struck your heart
that hasn't first gone through Mine.

I have inscribed your name on My hands (Isaiah 49:16)
and continue to bind you onto My heart. Please don't
doubt My love for you. Please know, from the bottom of
your heart, that every painful situation you have endured
thus far, I have experienced with you. And I have never
left you—nor will I ever leave you—to walk through any-
thing alone. As a loving parent who knows what's best for
His child, I have your utmost good in mind. And I will
continue to do so until you are finally safely home.

PART II:

Unraveling the Lies

*You shall know the truth, and the
truth shall make you free.*

JOHN 8:32

I'll Never Be Completely Healed
Re-examining the Healing Power of the Cross

Jean asked a lot of questions about forgiveness. She alluded often to regrets. And she had said, a few too many times, "I don't know why God would want *me*."

I finally pulled her aside and asked what was gnawing at her insides.

"I've done something I believe is unforgivable in God's eyes," she said.

I knew what it was before she said it. I knew because just about every woman who says that to me is suffering from the same pain of shame, guilt, and remorse. Jean was referring to her decision, years earlier, to abort her unborn child.

Prior to this pregnancy Jean had suffered a few miscarriages, and her doctor advised her to have an abortion because of possible health riskes to her or the baby. But now Jean regretted that she hadn't questioned or refused the doctor's advice. She was haunted by the thought that she gave in to the suggestion because it seemed the more convenient answer than going through with the pregnancy. She wished more than anything that she could take back that one decision, which had weighed heavily on her heart ever since.

"I *knew* it was a child," Jean said between tears. "But I rationalized it.

I tried to tell myself it was for the sake of my health. For some reason I went through with it. I *hate* myself for it. And even if God *can* forgive me, I can't forgive myself."

Jean continued to feed the wound by refusing to believe that the cross was enough.

I sat down with Jean and we talked about what Jesus had done on the cross for us. He paid a penalty for our sin that we could never pay. And that perfect sacrifice—His life and blood—for us, was enough to take care of every sin we've ever done, and every sin we will do in the future. When Jesus uttered His last words from the cross, "It is finished" (John 19:30), He meant it. It is *finished*. The debt is paid. The original Greek word Jesus used for "finished" was *tetelestai*—a merchant's term meaning to complete, execute, or discharge a debt. Jesus was saying that the debt for sin was paid in full. There is no balance owed. There is no retribution still sought. It is *done*. And to properly appreciate, respect, and revere what Christ accomplished on the cross is to recognize its complete sufficiency for healing in *every* area of our lives—including the wounds or mistakes we refuse to forgive *ourselves* for.

I gently took Jean's hand and told her, "As long as you continue to hold onto this and believe it is unforgivable, you are saying to God that His perfect plan to atone for the sins of mankind, His perfect sacrifice through His beloved Son, Jesus, was not enough to cover *this* sin. Do you actually think Jesus' death was not good enough for *you*?" She didn't like hearing me word it that way. But that's how she was thinking.

"But how do I forgive *myself*?" she asked.

"You let that sin go by acknowledging that the cross was enough."

Any of us can unknowingly undermine the healing power of the death and resurrection of Jesus Christ when we believe that something we have done is outside the realm of God's forgiveness. We are, in a sense, saying, "That doesn't apply to *me*. What Jesus did could not cover what I have done."

When we have such thoughts, we must remove ourselves from the equation and focus on the One who so adequately and sufficiently "heals the brokenhearted and binds up their wounds" (Psalm 147:3).

The Wounds We Carry

I know many women whose hearts still ache today from a decision to abort their child years—sometimes *decades*—ago. Some women carry the wound of adultery, wishing they could go back in time and undo the unfaithfulness that eventually unraveled their marriage. Some women hang on to deep regrets in the area of parenting, wishing they'd spent more time with their children when they were younger or that they had paid more attention to early warning signs in their children of drugs, alcoholism, emotional instability, or eating disorders.

Whether our wounds are directly related to our behavior (such as the case of adultery) or not (as in the case of a child's decision to rebel or to begin using addictive substances), we can take a step toward healing by surrendering our heartaches to the One who knows us inside and out. And we must refuse to believe that the wounds we brought on by our own actions or attitudes are less eligible for forgiveness and healing. God—in His grace and generosity—forgives, heals, and restores, regardless of how the pain came into your life.

In Scripture we read of King David, who is described as a man after God's own heart (Acts 13:22). He wrote many songs of love and praise to his God. Yet during a restless season in his life, he lusted after a woman who wasn't his wife and committed adultery with her. When he found out she was pregnant as a result of his infidelity, he conspired to kill her husband and take her as his wife quickly so he could cover up his wrongdoing. If that wasn't bad enough, this woman's husband wasn't only a soldier serving in David's army; he was one of David's "mighty men."[1] In other words the man David had killed in an attempt to cover up his sin was one of his best soldiers and closest allies.[2]

Betrayal all around. Murder—in cold blood. And for a while, David appeared to be okay with it. Until the day he realized just how much he had offended God. When God rebuked David through the prophet Nathan, God reminded David of all He had given him. He had rescued David from Saul, who wanted him dead. Then the Lord raised up David to become the new king over all of Israel and Judah. And then God said, "If all this had been too little, I would have given you even more."[3]

What conviction! David's heart was cut to the core.

When David realized how much he had hurt God's heart, he wrote a song out of his remorse—one that we ourselves can pray as we seek God's cleansing and desire to restore our relationship with Him. And whether it was giving up a child, abusing your body in some way, leaving or betraying a spouse, failing to honor a parent while he or she was still alive, or *whatever* still haunts you today, this song can represent the beginning of wiping *your* slate clean, removing your guilt, and restoring your relationship with God.

In Psalm 51, David prayed:

> Have mercy upon me, O God,
> According to Your lovingkindness;
> According to the multitude of Your tender mercies,
> Blot out my transgressions.
> Wash me thoroughly from my iniquity,
> And cleanse me from my sin (verses 1-2).

Confessions from the Heart

David started his prayer by acknowledging that God is merciful, loving, kind, and tender-hearted when we come to Him and acknowledge our sin.

> For I acknowledge my transgressions,
> And my sin is always before me.
> Against You, You only, have I sinned,
> And done this evil in Your sight—
> That You may be found just when You speak,
> And blameless when You judge (verses 3-4).

David called upon God's cleansing forgiveness while humbly admitting that his offense was sin—not just a mistake or an oversight, but an outright transgression against God. David also recognized that his biggest offense was not toward the other people involved, but to a holy and just God ("Against You, You only, have I sinned"). He was not saying it was only God who was offended, but it was *primarily* God whom he sinned against—the same God he shared close relationship with.

> Behold, I was brought forth in iniquity,
> And in sin my mother conceived me.
> Behold, You desire truth in the inward parts,
> And in the hidden part You will make me to know
> wisdom (verses 5-6).

David acknowledged not only that he sinned, but that his overall condition was one of an imperfect, sinful man. He humbled himself and admitted there was nothing good in him apart from the God he knew and trusted.

> Purge me with hyssop, and I shall be clean;
> Wash me, and I shall be whiter than snow.
> Make me hear joy and gladness,
> That the bones You have broken may rejoice.
> Hide Your face from my sins,
> And blot out all my iniquities (verses 7-9).

David realized that before he could experience joy again, he must have the cleansing from God that is required for the two of them to enjoy restored fellowship:

> Create in me a clean heart, O God,
> And renew a steadfast spirit within me.
> Do not cast me away from Your presence,
> And do not take Your Holy Spirit from me.
> Restore to me the joy of Your salvation,
> And uphold me by Your generous Spirit.
> Then I will teach transgressors Your ways,
> And sinners shall be converted to You (verses 10-13).

Then David asked God for the removal of his sense of guilt and an ability to praise Him publicly once again:

> Deliver me from the guilt of bloodshed, O God,

The God of my salvation.
And my tongue shall sing aloud of Your righteousness.
O LORD, open my lips,
And my mouth shall show forth Your praise (verses 14-15).

Finally, David provided a glimpse of what God is really asking for when we have offended Him. He acknowledged that God doesn't want a great performance or a promise to be better. He doesn't want more money in the offering plate on Sunday morning or more of a concentration on good works so we can prove our worth to Him. God wants our *brokenness*—He wants our hearts to be truly crushed at our offense toward Him so that we never want to hurt Him that way again.

For You do not desire sacrifice, or else I would give it;
You do not delight in burnt offering.
The sacrifices of God are a *broken* spirit,
A *broken* and a *contrite* heart—These, O God, You will
not despise. (verses 16-17, emphasis added)

I love how *The Message* paraphrases David's heartfelt prayer of confession. See if you can relate to the passion expressed in this paraphrase (which seeks to deliver the flavor of the original Hebrew in which this song was written):

Generous in love—God, give grace!
    Huge in mercy—wipe out my bad record.
Scrub away my guilt,
    soak out my sins in your laundry.
I know how bad I've been;
    my sins are staring me down.
You're the One I've violated, and you've seen
    it all, seen the full extent of my evil.
You have all the facts before you;
    whatever you decide about me is fair...
God, make a fresh start in me,
    shape a Genesis week from the chaos of my life.
Don't throw me out with the trash,

or fail to breathe holiness in me.
Bring me back from gray exile,
    put a fresh wind in my sails!...
Going through the motions doesn't please you,
    a flawless performance is nothing to you.
I learned God-worship
    when my pride was shattered.
Heart-shattered lives ready for love
    don't for a moment escape God's notice
(verses 1-4,10-12,16-17).

As you read through David's prayer perhaps you thought of some of the ways you have offended God too. Or, maybe your hurt was someone else's doing, but you have held onto bitterness in your heart as a result. Maybe you're even thinking this is a good prayer for *someone else* to pray in seeking God's forgiveness for what they have done to *you*. But God wants your heart to be humble and broken before Him, asking for His cleansing and His purifying so you are clean from the inside out— whether it be for actions of your own doing that have caused you pain, or for *reactions* you've had as a result of the pain someone else caused.

Finding Your Song

Not only do we confess our sin so we can please God and restore our relationship with Him, we confess our sin so we will be healthy.

In another song, David talked about how our wounds fester when we keep them hidden, especially when those wounds are a result of our poor choices, our rebellion against God, or our selfish desires.

In Psalm 32, David wrote:

Blessed [or happy] is he whose transgression is forgiven,
Whose sin is covered.
Blessed is the man [or woman] to whom the LORD does
    not impute iniquity,
And in whose spirit there is no deceit.
When I kept silent, my bones grew old

Through my groaning all the day long.
For day and night Your hand was heavy upon me;
My vitality was turned into the drought of summer
(verses 1-4).

David was saying that when he refused to open his heart before God and confess what was there, he felt like he had lost his youth, his vigor, his energy to get through the day. He felt guilt weighing him down; he felt drained.

Then look at what happened when David finally confessed:

I acknowledged my sin to You,
And my iniquity I have not hidden.
I said, "I will confess my transgressions to the Lord,"
And You *forgave the iniquity of my sin*
(verse 5, emphasis added).

A couple verses later, David sang:

You are my hiding place;
You shall preserve me from trouble;
You shall surround me with songs of deliverance (verse 7).

David started out hiding his sin from God and trying not to think about the resulting trouble it had caused. But then he ended up hiding *himself* in God and looking to Him as the One who could *preserve* him from future trouble.

Did you catch what happened? David started out by holding within himself that which was hurting him physically and emotionally. As a result, he felt drained and defeated, weighed down by guilt and shame. So he gave his brokenness and pain to God and found himself forgiven and surrounded with "songs of deliverance" rather than sorrow and shame.

When you give God your self-inflicted brokenness, He surrounds you with songs of deliverance, like this one:

As far as the east is from the west,
So far has He removed our transgressions from us
(Psalm 103:12).

That means God doesn't define you by your sin. He doesn't see that sin hanging over your head every time you try to speak to Him. He doesn't remember that sin or bring it back in front of you when you do something else that offends Him.

He removes it. *It is finished.* It is wiped away. It is done.

Now, *that* is a song of deliverance. It's a song of liberty. And it's a song that has brought freedom to Jean's heart and home.

After my heart-to-heart talk with Jean about how God sees her as forgiven when she confesses her sin to Him, I cut out little pink hearts and wrote "Psalm 103:12" in the center of each one and put them all over Jean's house—on a small wooden cross on the wall of her living room, on her refrigerator door, on a picture frame by her phone. And in case that wasn't enough, I wrote "As far as the east is from the west" on a heart and put it in her Bible so she would remember that "as far as the east is from the west," so far has He removed her sins—even *that* sin—from her.

Binding Up Our Wounds

Sometimes we remain in a state of hurt or shame because we think of Jesus' death and resurrection in terms of how they rescue us from eternal condemnation, but we fail to realize the incredible significance His death and resurrection have for us as we continue life in the here and now! A prophecy in the Old Testament book of Isaiah, foretelling Jesus' death on the cross, gives us insight into what Jesus accomplished through His sacrifice. He not only secured the eternal salvation of all who would put their faith in Christ alone, He also provided the healing and wholeness necessary for us to be called His children—"and if children, then heirs—heirs of God and joint heirs with Christ" (Romans 8:17). Christ's death on the cross didn't just provide for your *eternal* life, it provided healing for your *everyday* life.

Here's what Isaiah prophesied:

> Surely he has *borne our griefs*
> And *carried our sorrows;*
> Yet we esteemed Him stricken,

Smitten by God, and afflicted.
But He was *wounded for our transgressions,*
He was *bruised for our iniquities*;
The chastisement for our peace was upon Him,
And by *His stripes* we are *healed*
(53:4-5, emphasis added).

Let me expound upon these verses so you thoroughly understand all that Jesus accomplished for you when He suffered and died to heal you physically, spiritually, and emotionally.

1. **He has *borne* your griefs**—The Hebrew word for "borne" in this verse means "to lift" or "bear with sorrow." And the word for "griefs" can also refer to malady, anxiety, or calamity, including disease, grief, or sickness. This verse is saying that Jesus took upon Himself to bear with sorrow everything you could possibly bear—physically, mentally, emotionally, and spiritually—on this earth. *So there is nothing that He is unfamiliar with when it comes to your pain—whether it resulted from your own sin or not.*

2. **He has *carried* your sorrows**—The word "carried" refers to a burdensome load that requires strong labor. This wasn't just an "I know how you feel" platitude. It was an "I've carried that for you and I know exactly how much it weighs" type of empathy!

3. **He was *wounded* for your transgressions**—This verse literally means He was "profaned" for your "revolt" or rebellion against Him. He was the scapegoat for all you have done and will ever do to deserve the punishment and death that He willingly took upon Himself. We know He did this willingly because later, in verse 7, we are told that Jesus "was led as a lamb to the slaughter, and as a sheep before its shearers is silent, so He opened not His mouth." He didn't kick or fight back or resist when taking all of this upon Himself for you. He was wounded *willingly* for you.

4. **He was *bruised* for your iniquities**—The word "bruised" means "to crumble" or "to beat to pieces." That's what Jesus endured to clear you of continued sorrow and eternal punishment. His body and His reputation were crumbled so you won't have to be.

5. **He has *healed* you through His stripes**—By His "stripes" or "black and blueness" you are "healed"—which, in this sense, means mended, cured, repaired, and thoroughly made whole.[4]

I love how the statement of healing in each verse is given in the past tense, even though Isaiah proclaimed these prophetic words several hundreds of years *before* Jesus came to earth. He didn't say, "He *will be* wounded for our transgressions" and "By His stripes we *will one day* be healed." Rather, God chose to use the past tense. Not only was Christ's work on the cross predestined before time and carried out according to God's will, but God saw it as *already done*. And, my friend, speaking today, not only has He *already* done these things on the cross, but the benefits are *already* carried out for you and me.

Jesus has *already* borne the grief you are experiencing today. He has *already* carried your sorrow—further than you will ever be expected to carry it. He has *already* healed and mended you through the wounds He received on your behalf.

Think about that. The grief you are suffering as a result of loss has already been borne by Jesus. The sorrows you are feeling from a broken heart have *already* been carried by Him. The wounds you so want healed have *already* been taken care of. And just as this wounded Jesus came up out of the grave with glorious scars to show us that He could conquer sin and its devastating effect on our life, you too can experience new life and a glorious testimony of what He has done through you.

Healing for Today

In Luke 4:18 we read that Jesus stood up in the temple and read a portion of the prophecy of Isaiah 61 and proclaimed that He was the

One about whom the prophecy was written. Reading from verses 1-2, He said:

> He has sent Me to heal the brokenhearted,
> To proclaim liberty to the captives
> And recovery of sight to the blind,
> To set at liberty those who are oppressed...

Jesus' work on the cross wasn't solely about saving you from eternal torment after you die and giving you a beautiful home in heaven someday. His work on the cross included healing you of every affliction you have experienced, every wound you have ever incurred, and every teardrop you have ever shed as a result of living in this corrupt and sin-ravaged world.

When the perfect Son of God gave His life on the cross, His perfect sacrifice was not only imputed to us and recorded on our account, but His life was transferred to us as well.

In the apostle Paul's proclamation in Galatians 2:20, we discover that our lives are no longer our own once we've received Jesus' atoning death for our sins and trusted in Him for our salvation. We are, instead, given the life—and healing and wholeness—of Jesus:

> I have been crucified with Christ; it is no longer I who live,
> but Christ lives in me; and the life which I now live in the
> flesh I live by faith in the Son of God, who loved me and
> gave Himself for me.

Read that verse again. It means your real identity, as a child of God, is no longer that of a wounded woman. She died with Jesus on the cross. That woman who still has regrets is no longer you. She went into the grave with Jesus when she asked for His forgiveness, and she came up out of the grave with a new, forgiven, regenerated life. The life you now live is the life of a whole and regenerated woman who is fully identified with Christ.

I encounter many women today who refuse to believe they will ever be whole this side of heaven because of certain painful experiences they've lived through. Wound after wound has cumulatively had the effect of shattering their security and confidence, or a series of horrific events has, from their perspective, traumatized them beyond repair.

If you are one of those women, please come with me to the foot of the cross. Then admit that every emotionally painful situation you've encountered, every physical or emotional wound you've received, is a result of the sin in this world, sin from another human being, or sin in your way of thinking and behaving. And that sin was atoned for at the cross. That sin was remedied, reconciled, and removed from your being through your trust and surrender to Christ. There, at the cross, Jesus made available to you the healing your soul longs for.

Our First Response

So if the healing lies in the cross, why is it we don't seek it there? I believe we, as imperfect humans, naturally go everywhere else to find the healing that only God can provide.

In her book *Lies Women Believe,* Nancy Leigh DeMoss says:

> When we are hurting, we are quick to turn to tangible resources in search of comfort, relief or escape. After all, it is a lot easier to call a friend for sympathy than to get on our knees with an open Bible and listen to what God wants to say to us…It is a lot easier to try to mask the pain with excessive food or sleep than to choose to deny our flesh and walk in the Spirit…It is easier to pay for a refill of Prozac than to ask God to show us if we have an ungrateful, demanding or bitter spirit. These means may provide a measure of relief, but they are likely to be inadequate and short-lived. Nothing less than the "God of all comfort" can meet our deepest needs at such times.

DeMoss continues, "This is not to say that all those other things are wrong." She explains that a good night's sleep and a change in diet can greatly affect our physical well-being, which in turn affects our emotional and mental well-being. Counselors, therapists, or friends can provide encouragement, especially if they help point our thinking back to the truth. A doctor may be able to detect and help correct a physical problem that is having an impact on our emotional condition.

"But," she says, "our tendency to look to professionals and pills to solve what, in many cases, are problems of the soul and spirit has left millions of women overmedicated, financially broke, disillusioned, and no better off than when they started."[5]

Nancy and I are not saying that seeking counseling, therapy, or medication is necessarily a result of lacking faith in Jesus' ability to heal your life. God often works through others to touch our lives and impart in us what we may be unable or unwilling to hear or learn anywhere else. We need other people—a community of believers—to help us confront issues in our lives and remain accountable. But please don't automatically assume medication is necessary for healing simply because Jesus' touch on your life wasn't enough. Make sure you have carefully explored all the possibilities and received experienced counsel.

The Healing in the Cross

Christina, whose story of being raised in the drug business is told in chapter 3, said she realized that true healing and freedom—from childhood hurts and the poor choices she made during her college years—came through her study of the Word of God, where she developed a true understanding of the message of the cross.

"I went through counseling," Christina said. "I saw doctors, tried medication. None of that worked. None of it was effective. I needed the Word of God. A love and insatiable appetite for the Word of God began to grow in me, and that's where I found victory...in the message of the cross."

So did Ivonne. So did Sharon. And so did Jean. They have all experienced the complete healing of Jesus that was made possible through His death and resurrection. And the remarkable news is that this healing and freedom they have experienced is *already* available to you.

Step #4 *Toward Healing and Wholeness*

Re-examine—and receive—the healing power of Jesus' death
for you on the cross.
*It was enough to heal the very deepest of your wounds—
including the self-inflicted ones.*

LET THE HEALING CONTINUE

1. The Bible tells us of a woman who was considered incurable by the medical professionals of her day. Yet something extraordinary happened when Jesus touched her. Read Mark 5:24-34 and thoughtfully answer the following questions:

    a. Was the woman healed immediately or gradually?

    b. What was the woman's response (note the end of verse 33)?

    c. What did Jesus say was the reason for her healing?

    d. Is it time to tell Jesus "the whole truth" about something in your life that has been plaguing you? Do that now in prayer.

2. Read John 9:1-12 and answer the following questions:

    a. Was the man's blindness healed immediately or was there a process?

    b. What did the man have to do to be healed?

c.   What might God want you to do before He brings healing? (Think in terms of honesty, accountability, obedience, and so on.)

3.   Read James 5:13-16.

a.   What does this passage tell us about the community of believers and how God uses them?

b.   In what ways can you call upon your church or small group to help you in your time of need?

4.   Using Psalm 51 as a guide to prayer, confess to God the things you've hidden in your heart. If you feel comfortable doing so, write out your prayer or confession here.

A Prayer of Healing

Precious Lord, examine me from the inside out. I truly want to be whole and complete in Your eyes. But that means letting You shine Your light on the darkness within…the shame that I hide, the resentments that plague me, the fears that seek to overtake me at times. God, I want to live in Your light as a confident, capable child of Yours. But to do that I must be free of the things I have yet to forgive myself for. Bring to my awareness what I am still holding onto and help me to release it to You, understanding and accepting that what You did for me on the cross was enough to remove it from my life and restore me to wholeness.

Thank You that You make all things possible—including redeeming and restoring someone like me. I present to You my heart and trust that You will hold it carefully as You cut out what needs to go, soothe the pain that needs tending to, and treat the disease of any lingering sin and self with Your refining fire. Lord, remove from me any bitter root that needs to be dissolved. Break down any walls of resentment or doubt. Drain any pools of guilt or shame so I can be whole and complete in You. May I be a walking testimony of the power of Your healing and hope.

That's Just the Way I Am

Receiving a New Identity

For years, Natasha lived in bondage to her fears without even realizing it.

She knew her husband loved her, but she was consumed with fear and anxiety that one day he would abandon her.

"I constantly doubted his faithfulness even though there was no logical reason to think this," she said. "I would continually probe him with accusatory questions that attacked his character. I tried to control whom he associated with. I found that I couldn't trust him no matter how hard I tried and how much I cried out to God."

Natasha found herself miserable, and unintentionally jeopardizing her marriage. "I knew God was all-sufficient to meet the needs of my heart. I knew God would never leave me or fail me, but this wasn't translating to how I lived out my life. I was very insecure and desperate for my husband to meet these needs."

This went on for a number of years until Natasha finally told God she was tired of talking to Him about her issues and not seeing any resolution in her life.

"I told God we're finished talking about it. I'd just continue to live out my life with the way things were."

We get that way sometimes, don't we? We get so tired of dealing with hurtful issues in our lives and wondering when the healing is going to happen that it's easier to just resign ourselves to the problems our wounds are causing and conclude that nothing will ever change.

Do you ever find yourself saying, "That's just who I am," or "That's just the way it's going to be"? The problem with this kind of white-flag surrender is that it prevents us from exploring further and asking the questions that could bring help: Why is this wound in my life? What is the root cause of it? What does God need to heal in my life for this fear to lose its hold on me?

Even Natasha admitted, "This was a very sobering place to be. I was choosing to take a defeated stance and gave up trusting God to meet me where I was."

She found herself defeated and depressed. In her mind she kept asking, *How did my marriage of 25 years erode to such a point?* And *How did I get into such a warped frame of mind?*

Uncovering the Wound

Like many of us today, Natasha had unresolved wounds in her heart—issues from her childhood she had never acknowledged or dealt with. She was strapped with lies that had accompanied her for years that she continued to believe. She had labels attached to her that she had never bothered to remove. Especially damaging was the fact Natasha had made the mistake of believing the lie, *That's just who you are, and you'll never change.*

We all have defining moments in our lives that can greatly influence who we become and which direction we choose to go. For Natasha, that defining moment came when she was five years old. She watched paramedics carry her father out of her family's living room on a stretcher and felt very much alone. Her mother, who had been absorbed with her father's illness and taking care of a baby with a life-threatening illness, had emotionally pulled away from Natasha to deal with the dying people in her life. So the day her father died, it was as if Natasha had lost *two* parents…and she felt desperately alone. No one assured her they would be with her. No one comforted her in her sadness.

"As I stood on the sidelines of this family I absorbed feelings of fear, anxiety, uncertainty, insecurity, and instability. And, although I didn't know it at the time, I began to construct a belief system riddled with lies such as *I'm alone. I'm not important. I'm unlovable. There's something wrong with me.*"

That insecurity, along with a fear of death, drove Natasha to accept Christ as her Savior at eight years old. But she accepted Him out of her need for a "Father" and didn't understand she needed a Savior as well. She longed for a father from whom she would never be separated, and God's promise to be her Father throughout eternity and never leave her was something she couldn't resist. But though she placed her trust in God for *eternal* life, Natasha didn't realize she could also trust Him with her *emotional* life. And she ended up taking those feelings of insecurity and instability into her young adulthood. During her last two years of high school and first years of college, she became involved with a man who gave her the attention she craved.

"But what I thought was love was really about lust. I gave him my heart, mind, and body. My weak boundaries caused me to lose my identity in this guy and the relationship deteriorated into an unhealthy dependency.

"That should have been a major red flag that things weren't right in the depths of my soul, but I didn't get it. What came out of this was a vow to avoid relationships with men so I wouldn't get hurt again."

She managed to do that for seven years, during which time she gained a sense of her own depravity and knew how much she needed a *Savior*, not just a heavenly Father. "I wanted to love Jesus with all my heart. I then became involved in Bible study and Christian ministry."

A few years after college, Natasha married Tim, a longtime friend who shared her vision for serving God. Although it was a comfortable, familiar relationship for her, she kept her heart guarded.

"I couldn't unreservedly give myself to loving him," she said. Unknowingly, she was still dealing with wounds from her past. She was afraid of being abandoned.

Several years after becoming a mother, Natasha invited her own mother, due to unforeseen circumstances, to move in with her family. But unresolved issues between the two of them quickly deteriorated their relationship. Believing her mother disapproved of how she was raising her children, Natasha pulled away from her mother to avoid the criticism. In her attempt to protect herself from hurt, Natasha unknowingly ended up doing the same thing to her mother that she believed her mother did to her as a child.

Feeling that God was disappointed with her because she had failed to make amends in her relationship with her mother, Natasha settled into a deep depression. She got to the point where she couldn't function or get out of bed. Her wounds left her feeling there was no way out. Desperate to be healed of her hurt, she cried out to God.

"It seemed like my prayers were hitting a brick wall. When I picked up my Bible to read it, God's words were no longer 'living and active' to me. It was the worst feeling to not have any sense of God's presence with me. I told Him I could endure *anything* as long as I had an awareness of His presence."

One night she dreamed she was sitting in a large auditorium surrounded by friends, family, and strangers. On the stage was Jesus, who was standing next to a large banquet table. He came out into the audience, walked up to Natasha, and invited her to go with Him to His banquet table. He said to her and everyone else present, "This is one whom I love and I invite her to eat with Me. I prepared this table to honor her." Natasha said her dream was a vivid picture of Psalm 23:5 ("You prepare a table before me in the presence of my enemies").

A New Sense of Hope

"I woke from that dream with an assurance of His love for me and a renewed sense of hope," Natasha said. "I got out of bed that day and began healing from my depression."[1] Natasha had decided to believe that Jesus really wanted her, even though she felt most of her life that no one else did. She then immersed herself in Bible study to further get to know—and trust—this God who loved her and promised to never leave.

As Natasha began to experience a restored relationship with God, she was able to experience restored relationships with her mother and husband too.

"Very slowly I took baby steps back toward my mom. We learned to genuinely forgive each other. Over the next five years, I saw God bring about reconciliation in our relationship."

God restored Natasha's relationship with her husband as well, through a process of prayer and reflection on Scripture.

"My husband began a job where he traveled a great deal. To me this seemed like a hotbed for potential infidelity. I couldn't handle the thought of that so I coped by, again, emotionally withdrawing. We had moved to another state. With my support network removed from me and him traveling so much, I was very lonely."

Natasha became a part of a year-long group at her church that was studying the Christian disciplines of prayer, fasting, meditation, and solitude.

"It seemed to me that every discipline was all about listening to God, hearing His voice, and following His promptings. I realized I had lost that kind of interaction with God somewhere along the way. I told God if He would just talk to me I would follow through with whatever He showed me."

As Natasha began to practice the disciplines of prayer and reflection on God's Word, she gained insight into the ways she had been operating in relationships all of her life. She realized that she truly believed that everyone she loved would leave her and they would do this because there was something wrong with her. This intense fear of abandonment was deeply affecting her relationships and, as a result, she became either too consumed in a relationship or isolated. She couldn't find a balance.

"I developed many different sin patterns. The ones that wreaked the most havoc on my family were my acute anxiety over the fear of losing them and the control I tried to exercise over things and people to keep that from happening. My kids resented my overprotective tendencies and my husband resented my scrutinizing his every move."

For Natasha to acknowledge the behavior patterns that resulted from her wrong thinking was a big first step toward recovery. Her next step was to seek healing, no matter what it cost.

Taking the Next Step

The step that made all the difference for Natasha was choosing to believe God *wanted* to give her freedom from the bondage she was in. So she began to pray for that freedom.

"I prayed daily that I would allow God to work on my heart and heal me, and that my fear, unbelief, and hard heart would not interfere and overtake the work He wanted to do in my life. I prayed I would have the courage to walk through any door to healing that He put before me."

This commitment to pray for freedom was another critical step forward in Natasha's healing process. She believed God wanted her to confess her fears and anxieties to other Christians whom she could trust and to ask for their prayer support. She also participated in a reflective prayer session at her church that focused on emotional healing through prayer and accountability.

During a reflective prayer session, Natasha focused on her fear of being left alone. She remembered standing in her living room, as a five-year-old, and watching as the paramedics carried her dad out of her home on a stretcher.

"The whole memory was very disturbing to me. It hurt a lot. I was so sad and confused. I believed I was alone in that moment. When we prayed about what truth God wanted me to understand in that moment of my life, I had a very visual picture in my mind of Jesus standing there with me feeling the same sadness. These are the words that came to my heart: 'I know this hurts you, Natasha, but I will stay close to you.' Immediately I felt this huge flood of relief and the aloneness and sadness left. I thought later those were the very words I needed someone to have said to me at the time. I needed someone to validate how much it hurt and I needed someone to assure me that they would be there with me. Since Jesus was now the one who had done that, everything felt all right.

"Now when I think about God never leaving or forsaking me, I can really believe it. *All my life* I knew that verse in my head ["He Himself has said, 'I will never leave you nor forsake you'" (Hebrews 13:5)], but in that moment it finally transferred to my heart. Now that this truth was embedded in my heart, an amazing transformation began to take place. I began to relate differently to my husband. I couldn't even begin to feel that fear of abandonment by him anymore. I didn't feel compelled to know every detail of his day. I wasn't churned up inside by these things anymore. I could trust him and God."

When Natasha learned to trust that God would never leave her, she was able to trust that her husband—and others—wouldn't either. When she realized that loving God was not a risk, she realized she could love others, too, regardless of the risk.

Natasha's husband has been astonished by the difference in how she now relates to him. And she herself is astonished at how God has opened her heart and enabled her to love her husband and others like never before.

Natasha said it wasn't the dream years earlier and the feeling of Jesus' presence during her reflective prayer session that had the biggest impact on her life. Those were emotional experiences that we all want, and we often want them immediately. But emotional experiences are rare, and when we *seek* an emotional experience we contradict the very thing that pleases God—placing our simple trust and faith in Him (Hebrews 11:6). It was, rather, the daily prayer and Scripture reading year after year that kept the soil of Natasha's heart prepared for the Holy Spirit to do a healing work in her. That daily prayer and Scripture reading, she said, was crucial to moving past the mind-set of "That's just the way I am" to "This is who I am in Christ."

Natasha had to leave behind her old way of thinking and seek out her new identity in Christ. That new identity said she was not an unwanted, insignificant, abandoned child. She was, instead, loved by God, who had always loved her and promised to never leave her. And therefore, she had no reason to fear abandonment by Him or anyone else.

Your Real Identity

Any one of us can find ourselves feeling stuck when it comes to unresolved wounds in our lives and an eventual inability to move forward spiritually. But the common element in breaking free from the bondage of our past is seeing ourselves not in light of our past circumstances, but in light of our present condition. We must learn to see ourselves as God sees us—the new regenerated woman, not the old wounded one.

Believing what God says about you takes more than just positive thinking. It takes faith—faith to believe that when He says you are a new person in Him, He means it.

God's Word says that when you place your trust in Christ alone for the forgiveness of your sin and for eternal life, you become His adopted child (John 1:12; Romans 8:14-17). And in that relationship as His child you have a new identity that does not include the corruption or chaos of your past, or the problems in your present, or the fears of your future. In your new identity, God calls you...

- *His child*—John 1:12 says, "As many as received Him, to them He gave the right to become children of God, to those who believe in His name."

- *His friend*—Jesus said, "No longer do I call you servants, for a servant does not know what his master is doing; but I have called you friends, for all things that I heard from My Father I have made known to you" (John 15:15).

- *A saint*—In Ephesians 1:1, believers in Christ are called saints. *Yeah, but I'm not a saint,* you may be thinking. Your actions may not always say it. But your condition in Him says it. You are seen as perfect by Him because You are covered in the righteousness and goodness of Christ.

- *Forgiven*—Colossians 1:14 says you have been redeemed (bought back) and forgiven of all your sins—past, present and future. So your past sins—or wounds—can no longer define you. Your slate is wiped clean.

- *Complete*—Do you feel like a work in progress? Many women describe themselves this way, referring to how they are not yet what God desires of them. But God's Word is the final authority and it says "you are complete in Him" (Colossians 2:10). The work has *already* been done. You just need to live in that truth and wear it.

- *Secure*—both eternally and daily, in Him. You are free from condemnation (Romans 8:1-2), free from condemning charges (Romans 8:31-34), and free from the possibility of abandonment (Hebrews 13:5).

- *Unconditionally loved*—Romans 8:35-39 says *nothing* can separate you from the love of God—nothing! Not death, life, circumstances, sin, poor choices, or a season of rebellion.

- *His temple*—that means God lives within you. Your heart is His home. And He dwells with you daily (1 Corinthians 6:19).

- *Royalty*—He says you are seated with Him in the heavenly places (Ephesians 2:6).

- *His masterpiece*—He says you are His "masterpiece" created in Him for good works that He prepared for you before you were born (Ephesians 2:10 NLT).

- *Fully capable by His power*—God's Word says you are able to accomplish "all things" through Christ who gives you strength (Philippians 4:13).

- *His Possession*—God's Word says you are not your own; you belong to Him because you were "bought at a price" (1 Corinthians 6:20). That means He protects you and provides for you as His own. That also means nothing can touch you that hasn't first gone through His loving hands. (We will look more at this concept in the next chapter when we discuss your responsibility to the One who owns you.)

I'm Just That Way

The more you reaffirm who you are in Christ, the more your behavior will reflect your true identity. However, you can refuse to live in your new identity if you continue to see yourself in terms of your wounds. Have you ever heard a woman, or maybe even yourself, say:

- "I am an adult child of an alcoholic and therefore I struggle with certain dysfunctional behaviors. That's just the way I am."

- "I don't have any close friends because I've never trusted anyone enough to get close to them. That's just the way I am."

- "Because of what I've been through in my past, I've always been insecure."

- "I have abandonment issues. I'm just that way."

- "I've never had a lot of female friends. I don't trust them and I never will."

- "I've always needed a man in my life, and that will never change."

- "I hate being alone. It goes back to my childhood. I'm just that way."

- "I'll always worry when my children are out of my sight. That's just the kind of mom that I am."

- "I'm sorry I got so defensive. You should know I'm just that way."

Scripture directly refutes this way of thinking, telling you and me that when we are in relationship with Christ, we are no longer *that way*. The fears, issues, disabilities, doubts, and weaknesses that comprised your past identity have been dissolved, and you now possess the identity and character of Christ. As Galatians 2:20 says, "I have been *crucified with Christ*; it is no longer I who live [the old you was left at the cross with Christ], but Christ lives in me; and the life which I now live in the flesh [your identity today] I live by faith in the Son of God, who loved me and gave Himself for me" (there's your new identity—loved and redeemed). Got it? The old you is gone. The new you has taken on the identity and characteristics of Christ.

Second Corinthians 5:17 says if you are in relationship with Christ, you are a "new creation; old things have passed away; behold, all things have become new." That means old behaviors, insecurities, anxieties, bad habits, doubts, fears, an inability to trust, and other issues from your past are gone. And the new you operates in the love, joy, peace, patience, kindness, goodness, faithfulness, gentleness, and self-control that are evidence of the Holy Spirit's control of your life (Galatians 5:22-23).

And yet we all have moments when we slip back into the old life, the old wounds, the old issues, the old behaviors.

Mary's New Identity

In Scripture we read of a woman named Mary Magdalene who was among Jesus' close followers. Contrary to common myths, legends, and misunderstandings, she was *not* the woman caught in adultery (John 8:1-12), nor was she the unnamed "sinful woman" in Luke 7:37-38 who anointed Jesus' feet and wiped them with her hair. All we know of her past, before she met Jesus, is one descriptive line that is full of implications. Scripture defines her as the one "out of whom had come seven demons" (Luke 8:2).

Wow! This woman was not possessed by one, but *seven* demons. Talk about a rough past! What I find interesting about her is that there is no indication in her life, once she met Jesus, that she was enslaved, provoked by, haunted by, or resigned in any way to her past. In other words, when Jesus healed her of her demonic state, she didn't continue to have issues.

As Mary followed Jesus' ministry (Luke 8:1-3) we don't read that she had a difficult time when Jesus cast out demons from others because it was too close of an issue to her. We don't read of her having to leave the scene or being majorly distraught when Jesus came into contact with other demoniacs who sought to be delivered. We don't have any accounts whatsoever of fear or anxiety on her part when she was exposed to issues that were "too close to home" for her.

We do know, however, that on the third day after Jesus' death, Mary Magdalene was part of a group of women who set out early to go to Jesus' tomb. This woman didn't stay away because "going near dead people would really bother me because of what I've been through in my past." She wasn't convinced that "because of my past, I just can't handle being around the tombs." All of the "demons from her past" were gone, literally and figuratively. She no longer lived in fear, shame, or harassment from past issues. All we saw of her was her new life—one that was completely healed and committed to following Jesus.

Bible teacher John MacArthur says this about the behavior and healing of demoniacs:

> Evil spirits never voluntarily entered the presence of Christ. Nor did they ever knowingly allow one whom they possessed to come close to Him. They often cried against Him (Luke 4:34). They sometimes caused violent convulsions in a last-gasp effort to keep the wretched souls they possessed away from Him (Mark 9:20), but Christ sovereignly drew and delivered multitudes who were possessed by demons (Mark 1:34, 39). *Their emancipation from demonic bondage was always instantaneous and complete.*
>
> Mary Magdalene was one of them. How and when she was delivered is never spelled out for us, but Christ set her free, and she was free indeed. Having been set free from demons and from sin, she became a slave of righteousness (Romans 6:18). Her life was not merely reformed; it was utterly transformed.[2]

Do you have a past that you've broken free from, like Mary Magdalene? Or do you continue to let it haunt your circumstances or even dictate who you are today? When I find myself excusing my behavior because of past issues or saying something like "That's just the way I am," conviction always stabs at my heart and I'm reminded, once again, that Christ died for me to redeem *the way I am* so He can make me *more like Him.* When certain things from my past start to bother me, I have to ask myself, "Did Jesus take that away or not?" The truth is He did His part completely. I have to do mine. And my part is trusting that "old things have passed away; behold, all things have become new."

A Constant State of Crisis

Sometimes, however, we just don't let the old things go away. Just as we can ignore our true identity by saying, "I'm just that way," we can also ignore the blessings and newness in our life and fail to move forward by having the mind-set "*Life* is just that way."

Have you ever known someone who is in a constant state of crisis? One thing after another seems to happen on a continuous basis, leaving that person in a perpetual state of pain.

Nora was like that. Several years ago I met with her regularly for discipleship.

"How's it going this week?" I would ask.

"Well, you know, it's always a crisis," Nora would say.

By the third week, I challenged her answer.

"*Always* a crisis? *Really?* What do you mean?"

Between Nora's two adult children, one of whom was constantly running from the law, the other who was experiencing constant health problems as a result of methamphetamine use, and Nora's extended family, including brothers and sisters who were using drugs, fighting illness, or involved in some sort of scandal, Nora explained that every day was pretty much chaos.

"I've been around crises for so long I wouldn't know how to operate in a world where things went well," she said. And she wasn't being sarcastic. She'd become comfortable with her life as it was. It was what she expected. It was all she knew.

"What if every day were to be a blessing?" I asked her. She looked at me like I was crazy. I continued: "You're still alive, aren't you? Your kids are still alive. Your son is, by some miracle, not in jail right now. Your grandchildren are healthy. And what about the greatest blessing on earth? You have a personal relationship with the God of this universe and you are an heir of all that is." I took her through the book of Ephesians and reminded her of her spiritual inheritance and the fact that she has eternal life waiting for her.

Nora appeared encouraged by that and went home that day with a lighter spirit. But the following week, when I asked her how she was doing, she said, "Well, you know. Same old thing. Always a crisis."

Are you tired of the *same old thing*? I am. Christ died to *deliver* us from the same old thing. The same old sin. The same old habits. The same old excuses. The same old crises.

What if you and I were to deliberately focus each day on the blessings God has given us? I'm sure we'd find them. And then suddenly the *same old thing* would be replaced by a *great new thing*.

Leaving Crisis Mode

Fast-forward 15 years. I'm discipling a woman named Patti. No more than a year after she received Christ into her life she was diagnosed with ductal carcinoma. After being diagnosed, misdiagnosed, and then rediagnosed she learned she would have to have an immediate radical double mastectomy and breast reconstruction within the next four to six months to rid her body of the fast-growing cancer. While she was still processing that news, her husband, Scott, was injured on the job when a concrete wall fell on him and crushed several of his vertebrae, broke his wrist, and nearly killed or paralyzed him. After nearly a month in the hospital Scott was released, and then Patti entered the hospital for her surgery. Then while they were both still recovering, Scott lost his job, lost his father, and his mother suffered a stroke. Patti began to have a glazed-over look in her eyes.

"When's it all gonna stop?" she asked me, exasperated.

Then the day after she was baptized in our church, Patti texted me to let me know her parents had left town early because her father was suddenly experiencing a serious health problem.

"Just when things were starting to settle down, my dad has this health problem," she said.

Patti's comment got me to thinking about life in general. You know what? There will *always* be something in this world that can cause us to become fearful or upset. That's the world we live in. We're mortal, and so are the people around us. We age, and we experience injury, sickness, failing health, financial setbacks, disappointments, misbehaving or rebellious children, aging parents, annoying neighbors, threatened lawsuits, dying pets. We will always face circumstances that tempt us to feel that life is unfair, that we are being punished, that God is silent. But every difficult situation in this ever-changing world is yet another opportunity to hold on to our never-changing Lord.

I texted Patti, "There will always be something that keeps us clinging to God." Patti responded by saying she was applying Philippians 4:6 to her circumstances yet again: "Don't worry about anything; instead, pray about everything" (NLT).

She then followed up with one more message: "I was very upset yesterday but prayed about it and am relatively peaceful at this point. Thank you for the prayers."

Patti was learning, day by day, moment by moment, to trust God in the everyday occurrences of life. She is learning to call them that, too, instead of referring to everything as a crisis.

Did you catch the difference between Nora and Patti? Nora stayed in her constant state of crisis. She expected it. She felt comfortable there. She made her bed there. Why would she want to leave? *Crises had become part of her identity.* Patti, on the other hand, decided to live differently. She walked *out* of her world of crisis and into a world of hope. She focused her eyes on Christ, not her circumstances. *Her hope became part of her identity.*

Are you one who has hope? If all you have is this world, you will be undone by your circumstances and you will have no hope. But if you have Christ living in you, you have hope indeed. So live like it!

Let It Shape You

As you've read the stories of various women in this book, hopefully you're noticing a pattern. Ivonne no longer sees herself as a poor immigrant child of a dysfunctional family. She understands that she is a loved child of God with a bright and hopeful future. Sharon doesn't see herself as the evil, unwanted little girl that her father said would never be loved. Instead she sees herself as a daughter of the King and bursting with potential to live out His purposes for her. And Christina, who grew up in remote, lawless places and searched through dumpsters for food, now knows intimately the Bread of Life (John 6:48) and knows that she will never hunger again.

All these women will admit that the lies from their pasts still try to taunt them from time to time. But they have come to recognize the lies and replace them with the truth about their identity in Christ.

Christina says, "I've heard the lies: *You will never change. You will never be different.* I have to go back and say, 'Lord, I *know* I can be changed. I know I *have* been changed.'"

Getting a New Hard Drive

We can live in our new identity—instead of clinging to the old, wounded one—by asking God to "rewrite" our hard drive. It's on our interior hard drive to think a certain way, respond a certain way, behave a certain way. Sometimes it comes out when we least expect it. But it is something we must keep in check and surrender to the healing power of Jesus.

"Check yourself before you wreck yourself," Patti often says. And it's good advice. We must constantly be aware of those feelings and fears from our past that can creep into our present and distract us from who we are in Christ. Here's a way you can check yourself so your hard drive is representative of God's rewrite on your life:

1. Let Nothing Get in the Way of Your Healing

Christina, whose story is in chapter 3, said she had to deliberately determine to let nothing keep her from healing in order to finally be whole.

"For me not only is God able but He's *willing* to heal me. It's one thing to say 'He *can* do it.' But it's another to say 'He's *willing* to do it' and 'He *wants* to do it.' I had to be an active participant in that and say, 'There is nothing that is going to get in the way of His healing stripes. There is nothing that's going to get in the way of Him healing me. We must resolve to not opt out of our healing.'"

Christina said, "We are a society that thinks we can opt out—we opt out of prayer time, devotional time, Bible study, church, fellowship. If you want healing and desire it, there is no opting out."

As I've discipled women over the past 25 years, I've seen Christina's statement to be true. The women who seem to struggle the most with personal, emotional, and spiritual healing are the same women who are constantly opting out. They are the ones who can never seem to commit to a women's Bible study. They are the ones who are constantly unable to attend the workshop on spiritual growth or that yearly women's conference that significantly impacts the women who attend. They are the ones who come to my mind when I hold a women's study and think, *She should've been here for this.* I've come to realize through the years that the reason these women are the ones who "really needed that" is because they rarely put themselves in the position to receive God's healing by being in the places where healing happens.

If you are serious about healing, put yourself in the place where you can be healed. God often heals us in community. Get the accountability you need. Commit to—don't just attend—that small group Bible study. Make yourself vulnerable to those whom you can trust. Participate in a prayer group of people who care about you and will commit to praying for you as you commit to praying for them. Invest whatever it takes when it comes to your time, money, and effort. Let nothing keep you from Jesus' healing touch.

A woman in the Bible was willing to face public scorn, ridicule, possibly even punishment in her quest to touch Jesus and be healed, yet nothing would keep her from Him. She was desperate to be healed so she did what it took to receive Jesus' touch (Mark 5:25-34). Are you that desperate to be healed too? Then let nothing get in your way.

2. Listen for God's Voice

Healing comes when we see ourselves as God sees us. When we hear His voice and accept it as truth. And that happens through dialogue with God. This doesn't mean a monologue where we do all the talking. We must listen to what *He* is saying to us. Natasha had to be patient so she could "hear" God's voice. She spent time in His Word and in reflective prayer. Are you listening for His voice as well? If you are, you will hear what He wants to say. (For a clearer understanding of how to listen to God see the chapter "Listening to His Loving Voice" in my book *Letting God Meet Your Emotional Needs,* or find free articles on the subject at my website www.StrengthForTheSoul.com.)

3. Let God Define Who You Are

This happens when you understand His Word and what He says to you through the Scriptures. Be active in the Word of God; truly seek His face in His Word. He is the One who defines who you are—not your parents, not your past, not this world, not your wounds. In order to let God—and not the other voices we tend to hear—define us, we must learn to bring "every thought into captivity to the obedience of Christ" (2 Corinthians 10:5). When you hear negative thoughts defining you, take them captive and be determined to only hear the thoughts that are obedient to Him, the thoughts that are consistent with His Word's description of you.

Christina said her thoughts would attempt to take her down the dark path of her past and convince her of things that weren't true about her.

"I've never drank alcohol, but if I'm stressed, it is on my hard drive to say 'I need a drink.' I've had to kick out the wrong thoughts and take captive any stronghold that sets itself up against Christ and really be active in doing that."

God's definition of you will never accuse you in terms of your identity. It will only affirm you. You won't hear God say, "You will never be the kind of Christian you say you are," or "You are so dysfunctional just like everyone else in your family." Rather, He will say, "I have loved you with an everlasting love" (Jeremiah 31:3), and "You are the light of the world" (Matthew 5:14), and "You are not your own…you were bought at a price" (1 Corinthians 6:19-20). God's voice will convict our hearts when we are going astray, but will never condemn us. There is a huge difference.

Embracing the Truth

My friend, there may be days when you feel broken, devastated, bitter, and angry. There may be days when you feel like saying, "That's just who I am and I'll never change." There may be days when you say, like Natasha, "I'm tired of the same old pain with no change." But don't give up on the God who has already won the battle for you and promises to carry out the good work that He has started in you.

Regardless of how you feel, God's truth says you are a new creation. Don't let your feelings tell you otherwise. Don't let your opinions tell you otherwise. God's truth has everything to do with who you *really* are.

Jesus Himself said, "You shall know the truth, and the truth shall make you free" (John 8:32). Free from the feelings of guilt and shame that arise from a past that has already been erased. Free from the old tapes that run through your mind trying to drag you back to a life that is no longer yours. Free from feelings of inadequacy because of what you've been through. And "if the Son makes you free, you shall be free indeed" (John 8:36).

Do you know the truth of God's Word and what it says about who you *really* are? Do you believe that you are His child, His friend, His possession and heir of all that is? Believe the truth of what God has said about *you*. Believe it, embrace it, *live* it—and the truth will set you free.

STEP #5 *Toward Healing and Wholeness*

Renew your mind to think differently.

You have a new identity in Christ—and the old you that was "just that way" is gone.

LET THE HEALING CONTINUE

1. Jesus said "You shall know the truth, and the truth shall make you free" (John 8:32). List the truths about your identity (see the list on pages 98-99) and write them in the following format: "I am His child; I am His friend. I am…"

2. Now circle the ones above that have the most potential to set your heart free and ask God to plant into your heart that truth of who you are in His eyes.

3. Which of the phrases on pages 90-100 have you found yourself saying every now and then? (If yours isn't in the list, write it out here below. (You must first be aware of how you see yourself so you can let God change your focus.)

4. Now rewrite any of those phrases that you struggle with, keeping your new identity (from pages 98-99) in mind. (I have completed the first two for you.)

    • I am a child of God (John 1:12) and I have a Father who is perfect.
    • Jesus calls me His "friend" (John 15:15) and I can be the same kind of loving friend to others that He has been toward me.
    •

    •

    •

5. Read Mark 5:25-34 and answer the following questions:

    a.   How does Mark identify the woman prior to her meeting Jesus?

b. Read the story again. How would you identify this woman based on her actions and her response to Jesus (verses 27-28,33)?

c. What did Jesus call her in verse 34?

d. What did Jesus say to her and do for her?

6. Read John 8:1-11 and answer the following questions:

a. How would the woman in this passage typically be described? (What would her identity be in her village?)

b. What did the people think of her?

c. What was Jesus' reaction toward her?

d. What was her new identity after she met Jesus?

7. What do the above two exercises illustrate about one's identity once they meet Jesus?

8. What does that mean in terms of who you *think* you are as compared to who Jesus *knows* you are?

A Prayer of Praise for Your New Identity

Precious Savior, sometimes I forget the lengths You went to so You could secure a new identity for me. Forgive me for the times I slip back into the patterns of my past and think of myself as someone I used to be. Because of Your redeeming love, I am no longer that person. You have inscribed me on the palms of Your hands (Isaiah 49:16), and I know You will never forget what You have done for me. Help me to inscribe on my heart and mind what You have done for me so I will never forget that I am a "new creation; old things have passed away; behold, all things have become new"
(2 Corinthians 5:17).

I Have a Right to Be Happy

Revisiting the Meaning of Surrender

Jill Kelly—like all of us at one time or another—believed she had a right to be happy. Until she finally found peace through surrendering her rights.

Jill, the wife of Hall of Fame quarterback Jim Kelly, believed she was heading toward her happily-ever-after when she married football's most eligible bachelor in the spring of 1996. But her fairy-tale romance soon turned into a lonely marriage and what seemed like life as a single parent. When their son, Hunter James Kelly, was born a year later, their lives turned upside down.

At four months of age, Hunter, who was born on his father's birthday, was diagnosed with a fatal genetic disease called Krabbe leukodystrophy (Krabbe disease). With no treatment and no cure, this disease causes the body to eventually shut down. Jill was told her son wasn't expected to live beyond two years old, yet he courageously fought the disease for eight years, impacting thousands of lives in his daily, and sometimes moment-by-moment, struggle to live.

Jill struggled along with her son. As she endeavored to keep her son alive, care for her other two children, and make it through a difficult, loveless marriage, she cried out to God for healing for her son and hope for her marriage and family.

"Hunter's struggles drove me to my knees—and God, in His mercy, kept me there," she wrote in her account of Hunter's story.[1]

Instead of pleading with God for life to be different, Jill pleaded with Him to save her son and her entire family.

There were days she didn't believe she could face one more health problem her son was experiencing, one more injury he suffered from continual broken bones, or one more tear he cried from constant pain and discomfort.

And yet Jill knew the concept of surrender. She knew her life was not her own.

After her son passed away (on August 5, 2005), she and the entire family were devastated. But she was able to write in her book:

> So while it seemed to me that my faith had failed me, Jesus hadn't. It was in pursuit of that faith that I first met my Savior, Jesus Christ. And now in Hunter's death and my grieving, that faith had been tested. In the midst of my confusion and despair, I came to realize that God was faithful, even if through the fog of depression I was unable for a time to see and connect with Him.
>
> Slowly, ever so slowly, hope was nurtured back to life, my faith was renewed, and healing gradually began.[2]

In retrospect, Jill could see that not only did God have a purpose behind their pain, but He was working to heal all of them, in spite of Hunter's condition: "Maybe we needed to be healed more than Hunter did. What if Hunter's disease wasn't a tragedy but a triumph somehow? What we perceived as evil (surely, disease is evil), God used for good."[3]

Through their desire to raise awareness of the disease that took their son's life and provide hope and encouragement to other families experiencing the same pain as a result of the disease, the Kelly family established Hunter's Hope—an organization that confronts the critical need for information, awareness, and research in response to the threat of Krabbe disease and related leukodystrophies.[4] In addition, God brought reconciliation to the Kelly marriage and restored the Kelly family. Jill has authored several books and today shares her testimony for the glory of God.

"Happiness often depends upon our circumstances and expectations," Jill told me recently. "We have a tendency to put our hope and expectations in people (in particular, our husbands) and the things of this world and yet we are never fully satisfied. But the beauty of exhausting ourselves in the search is that, when those expectations are ripped to shreds, God is waiting. And where He is—in His presence— is fullness of joy. It's excruciatingly painful to go our own way and come up empty. Yet God allows us to seek and find what life looks like apart from Him so that only *His* love can find us and set us free."

Jill sees clearly now, in retrospect, that her life was never her own. And she lives with gratitude to the One who engineered her circumstances in the way that He did.

When I recently emailed Jill to thank her for her story that she so transparently told in her book *Without a Word*, praise for her Creator continued to roll off her tongue: "He really is indescribable, uncontainable...beyond comprehension. We wouldn't have a story if we were not rescued by the Greater Story!"

Can you and I say that? Can we say, "I wouldn't have a story at all if it weren't for His larger, greater story"? And, "I wouldn't have a life at all were it not for His divine intervention through my sorrow and suffering"?

Believing the Lie

When we believe we have a right to be happy, we're believing a lie that results in disappointment and disillusionment. Sometimes it even results in bitterness. But mostly it keeps us from a proper understanding of what it means to live as a follower of Christ.

There are two difficulties with believing the lie that we have a right to be happy.

Difficulty #1: We Are Not in Control

We live in a fallen world. Therefore injury, pain, disease, and tragedy are part of our existence—and they're all outside our control. We are also not able to control the actions and reactions of the people around us. You may decide you are going to enjoy a long life with the man you love, but he may decide otherwise. You may decide you want to be pregnant within a year of getting married, but then find yourself infertile. You may choose a certain career path, but find obstacles along the way and no job openings. Or you may decide you want to achieve certain physical goals and find that injury, health problems, or disease prevents you from doing so.

Difficulty #2: We Are Subject to God's Sovereign Will

We live in a world in which God is the supreme authority. We learned in the first three chapters of this book that God's will is sovereign. He will do what He desires in your life and the lives of others. And we cannot manipulate Him.

Given these two facts about life, we have but one alternative: to surrender to His sovereign will. When we surrender our lives to Jesus, we experience the joy that comes from living in quiet trust of our heavenly Father, who loves us and has promised to work all things together for our good (Romans 8:28).

Jill understood the concept of surrender. And she understands, today more than ever, that her life is not her own. Do you understand that as well?

Surrendering Your Will

Throughout the Bible we are told that if we call ourselves children of God, our lives are not our own.

In fact, we are told that we are *slaves*, with no rights at all. In the original Greek New Testament, the writers of Scripture used the word *doulos* to describe believers. Most of our English Bible translations render this to the word "servant," but the original Greek word actually means "slave."[5]

Now, I know you don't like the sound of that. Who wants to be someone's slave? But the Bible says we're *all* slaves—whether to sin or to righteousness. In Romans 6:17-18 we read this: "God be thanked that though you were slaves of sin, yet you obeyed from the heart that form of doctrine to which you were delivered. And having been set free from sin, you became slaves of righteousness."

We were born into slavery, having one master—sin. But Christ, through His death, redeemed us. He bought us out of our slavery to sin and death and made us slaves to Himself. And now we experience life—the life of freedom from sin, but also the life of slavery to a good and loving master, the Lord Jesus Christ.

Now you may be thinking, *No, Cindi! I am His servant. I serve Him willingly. I am* not *a slave.*

Yet John MacArthur made this observation in his book *Slave: The Hidden Truth About Your Identity in Christ*: servants are *hired*; slaves are *owned*.

> Servants have an element of freedom in choosing whom they work for and what they do. The idea of servanthood maintains some level of self-autonomy and personal rights. Slaves, on the other hand, have no freedom, autonomy, or rights. In the Greco-Roman world, slaves were considered property, to the point that in the eyes of the law they were regarded as *things* rather than *persons*.[6]

The New Testament scriptures say we are not our own, but we were "bought at a price" (1 Corinthians 6:19-20). We have been bought at a price—the blood of Christ—and therefore we have no rights to ourselves. We exist to serve and obey our Master, the Lord Jesus Christ.

Even Jesus made this clear when He taught about the priorities of our hearts and our loyalties: "No one can serve two masters; for either he will hate the one and love the other, or else he will be loyal to the one and despise the other. You cannot serve God and [money]" (Matthew 6:24).

The beauty of all this is that our Master is a good, loving master who wants the best for His slaves. In fact, He calls us His children.

Yet we often get this "rights" issue turned around. We tend to believe that as long as we obey God, He exists to serve *us* and grant us *our* desires. We think it is God's obligation to make us happy, grant our wishes, make our life fulfilling.

Jesus said in John 10:10 that He came that we "may have life, and have it abundantly."[7] But that life is in the context of obeying His greatest commandment, which is to love Him with all our heart, soul, and mind (Matthew 22:37), and to serve Him in obedience as a slave would serve his master.

Jesus even said that ultimately, our goal is to hear Him say, "Well done, good and faithful servant" (Matthew 25:23). And the original Greek word translated "servant" in that verse is, again, *doulos* —meaning "slave."

Service is a part of our role as God's possession, but it is not the extent of it. Our very lives belong to Him. Any rights we might have thought we had are His. So what does this have to do with our healing and wholeness?

When we understand properly who we are in relation to God, we cannot be disillusioned that "God is not answering my prayers." We cannot say, "God was supposed to bless my life." And we will not find ourselves saying, "Where is the benefit of serving Him?"

A slave has no rights. He or she depends only on the protection, provision, and generosity of the master.

My friend, if you would live from this day forward with the knowledge and affirmation that you are His, you belong to Him, and you owe your life to Him, suddenly your needs, wants, and expectations are no longer your concern; they are His obligation. In fact, your only concern is to please Him. That is the day your life is no longer about your rights, your disappointments, your hurts. It's about His redemptive work in you.

In Pursuit of My Happiness

I remember a time when I was holding onto certain expectations for my life, my marriage, my parenting, my ministry. Now there's nothing wrong with having expectations in relationships and goals in certain areas of life. But I was in a place where I was disappointed because I believed I had a right to more. I was looking for a formula to follow so I could receive God's blessings in the way that I expected. I also believed that if I pleased God I could be assured that others would respond to me in the way that I had hoped. As a result of feeling I had certain rights, I found myself frustrated and confused.

What am I doing wrong? I kept asking myself when a situation wasn't going the way I planned. *What did I do this time?* I asked myself, again, when I discovered I was the subject of criticism and gossip by a woman in my church. Eventually I found myself saying, "I don't have to put up with this" in an effort to "protect" my rights.

I finally spent some time on my face in prayer, asking God why I was so frustrated with everything and everyone around me. I asked Him to examine my heart and show me what needs to go from my life so I can experience *His* peace and joy. I then began reading through Jesus' words in John 15 and there I found comfort and hope:

> I am the true vine, and My Father is the vinedresser. Every branch in Me that does not bear fruit He takes away; and every branch that bears fruit He prunes, that it may bear more fruit...Abide in Me, and I in you. As the branch cannot bear fruit of itself, unless it abides in the vine, neither can you, unless you abide in Me.
>
> I am the vine, you are the branches. He who abides in Me, and I in him, bears much fruit; for without Me you can do nothing...If you abide in Me, and My words abide in you, you will ask what you desire, and it shall be done for you...
>
> As the Father loved Me, I also have loved you; abide in My love. If you keep my commandments, you will abide in My love, just as I have kept My Father's commandments and abide in His love.
>
> These things I have spoken to you, that My joy may remain in you, and that your joy may be full (verses 1-2,4-5,7,9-11).

I found in those verses not only comfort, but some insights as to why I was feeling so miserable:

1. Sometimes the pain we experience is really pruning.

Jesus didn't say, "Every branch that bears fruit I *punish*." He said every branch that bears fruit He "prunes, that it may bear more fruit" (verse 2). I was producing some fruit in my life, so I was confused about why I was hurting. But God apparently wants my life to produce *more* fruit, which comes about through a pruning of the attitudes, actions, and expectations in my life so that my character can be refined. I kept asking myself what I was doing wrong when instead I should have asked God, "How do You want to refine me?"

2. Without God, it's impossible to do anything.

Jesus wasn't kidding when He said, "Without Me you can do nothing" (verse 5). Sometimes we can fake it for a while by forcing a smile on our face and going through the motions at church or work, but if we are not abiding in Christ, we are not able to produce true fruit. This is so true for me, and I'm not just talking about ministry tasks. I don't function well as a wife, mother, daughter, sister, or friend when I am not abiding in Christ. If He is not the One I am looking to for my daily sustenance, I fail miserably in all that I attempt to accomplish. God truly wants me—and you, too—to be desperate for Him.

To abide means to continue with or to endure. Jesus was telling His followers to continue with Him, not to just pop in and out of the relationship when they needed something. If I am constantly in a place where I am depending on Him, I am abiding in Him in the same way a branch abides in the vine.

3. As I abide in Him, He hears me and provides for me.

We all have those times when we feel our prayers are bouncing off the walls. This is when I quote God's words back to Him, like those in John 15:7: "If you abide in Me, and My words abide in you, you will ask what you desire, and it shall be done for you." If I am desiring to be heard, desiring His peace, desiring His comfort, I ask myself, *Am I abiding in Him?* If so, He has promised He will hear me and grant me the petitions on my heart.

4. As I remain in Him, I experience His joy.

Jesus, as a result of His obedience to His heavenly Father, experienced the joy of perfect fellowship and unity with Him. He said we will experience that same joy when we are obedient to Him and remain in fellowship and unity with Him. When I am looking to what I want out of life, trying to control my circumstances and asking, "What am I doing wrong?" when it comes to achieving my desired results, I am not abiding in Him. I am, to the contrary, seeking my own will. But when I shift the focus and say, "How can I remain in You, Jesus?" I am putting myself in the place to be pruned, refined, and refreshed in His joy.

Resting in Him

Jill Kelly learned the secret of abiding in Christ. In a journal entry about a year before her son passed away (and in the midst of his continual decline in health), Jill wrote:

> Of all the gifts I'm most thankful for in this very moment, Lord Jesus, You're it. In this world with all its abundance, You are life to me. You are everything. You keep on giving; there is no end to Your grace and goodness. In You I am held together. Held together with a love that binds the parts of me that cannot function alone. If I rely on my brain, it will confuse me. If I rely on my body, I will fall apart. If I rely on other people, they will never meet my expectations. If I rely on my heart, it will bleed and break.
>
> When I look to You, Lord, and rely on You, I am whole and I can live. I am able to think with my brain, stand on my feet, love people for how You created them to be, and possess a heart that beats for You and allows me to go on. I know You hold Hunter. You hold our entire family. Thank You for Hunter. We trust You with every breath he takes. You give and You take away.[8]

In the midst of watching her beloved son suffer, Jill was able to praise God and exhibit a profound joy. It was because she knew what it meant to abide in Him no matter what life looked like. She "continued" with God as her sole source of strength, support, and encouragement.

Jill also knew that even though her life was not her own and she was God's bondslave, she was also loved.

First John 4:18 says "perfect love casts out fear." When we love God perfectly, we trust Him perfectly. And where there is perfect trust, there is no fear.

Trusting in His Love

Our description in the Bible as God's slaves is always in reference to our instruction in how to obey God and respond to His authority. But when it comes to our relationship with Him, God calls us His child, His heir, His beloved. Psalm 139 says that you are so special to Him that you were...

- Formed intricately in your mother's womb. (Verse 13 says you were not a cookie-cutter design. You weren't just run through the copy machine. You were intricately and carefully thought out and designed by Him personally.)
- "Fearfully and wonderfully" made. (In verse 14, God calls you "awesome.")
- Skillfully "wrought" in secret. (The Hebrew word for "wrought" in verse 15 means "to embroider" or carefully stitch. You are a very carefully put together bondslave of Christ's.)
- The subject of a story He has written about you. (Verse 16 says that before you were ever born, He had your whole life story written out.)

The Bible also says that God...

- Has precious thoughts of you that are too many to number (Psalm 139:17-18).
- Knows the number of hairs on your head (Mathew 10:30).
- Saves your tears in a bottle (Psalm 56:8), meaning He not only is aware of how many times you have cried, but He has kept your tears because they are so precious to Him.
- Has engraved you on the palms of His hands (Isaiah 49:16 NIV). He chose to keep the nail scars on His hands when

He went to the cross for you, meaning He chose a per-manent reminder of you on His body! It's an interest-ing fact that slaves were branded with their master's name to identify to whom they belonged. Yet Jesus chose to be "branded" with a remembrance of His love for *you*. How amazing is that?

So even though you as a slave don't have a right to make demands, you are in the hands of a God who loves you immensely and wants His best for you. I can rest in that. Can you?

When It Looks Like God Has Forgotten You

I know it's easy to sometimes feel that God has forgotten you, espe-cially when you look around and see others who are not living for God but appear to be doing better physically, emotionally, relationally, and financially. It's times like these when we feel we have a right to be happy, instead of watching someone else who hurt us live carefree.

"Margaret" (not her real name) recently complained to me that her ex-husband is a lot better off than she is financially, emotionally, and relationally, having found a new love after leaving her and her three children. "It's not fair," she said. "Why am I lonely and hurting while he is having the time of his life?"

Margaret and I talked at length about what her ex-husband is doing. While it may appear on the surface that he is "having the time of his life," his children no longer want him to be a part of their lives, and the day will come when he has to deal with the emotional and relational consequences of his actions. Margaret, on the other hand, has God's ear when she's hurting; finds comfort on lonely mornings by reading the Scriptures; and still has the love and loyalty of her children as well as the support of her family (and his!), their friends, and her local church family. Although Margaret can't necessarily see it yet, she is enjoying blessings today that her ex-husband may never again experience.

Asaph, one of the songwriters in the Bible, said that he "almost stumbled" when he looked at how others prosper while he suffered. But then he had to remind himself of the truth. Listen to his song and see if you can relate:

God is truly good to Israel,
    especially to everyone with a pure heart.
But I almost stumbled and fell,
    because it made me jealous to see proud and evil people
        and to watch them prosper.
They never have to suffer; they stay healthy,
    and they don't have troubles like everyone else.
Their pride is like a necklace,
and they commit sin
    more often than they dress themselves...
They sneer and say cruel things,
    And because of their pride, they make violent threats.
They dare to speak against God and to order
    others around...
Yet all goes well for them, and they live in peace.
What good did it do me to keep my thoughts pure
    And refuse to do wrong?
I am sick all day, and I am punished each morning.
If I had said evil things,
    I would not have been loyal to your people.
It was hard for me to understand all this!
Then I went to your temple, and there I understood
    (Psalm 73:1-6,8-9,12-17 CEV).

Did you catch Asaph's moment of truth? "Then I went to your temple."

When we look around at others and see they are wealthier or more comfortable than us, we may find ourselves disillusioned and believing that God hasn't been good to us. But when we focus our eyes on who God is, and His goodness to us, we regain a right perspective on things.

Toward the end of his song, Asaph sang,

Once I was bitter and brokenhearted...
But I never really left you, and you hold my right hand.
Your advice has been my guide
    and later you will welcome me in glory
    (verses 21,23-24 CEV).

Then listen to Asaph's expression of allegiance:

> In heaven I have only you,
>   and on this earth you are all I want.
> My body and mind may fail,
>   but you are my strength and my choice forever
>   (verses 25-26 CEV).

I love how Asaph realized—and sang about—the benefit of abiding with God in troubling times. He ended his song with this admonition:

> Powerful LORD God,
> All who stay far from you will be lost,
>   and you will destroy those who are unfaithful.
> It is good for me to be near you.
> I choose you as my protector,
>   and I will tell about your wonderful deeds
>   (verses 27-28 CEV).

When Asaph compared, he complained. But when he gained perspective, he praised.

Finding Your Joy

I think it noteworthy to mention that verse 25 of this song is a theme verse for Jill:

> Whom have I in heaven but You?
> And there is none upon earth that I desire besides You.

Jill includes that verse in her email signature and writes the reference, Psalm 73:25, next to her name when she signs her books. It's been my theme verse, too, through the years as I also realize that no one and nothing in this life will satisfy but Him.

Whom have I in heaven but You, O Lord, when I'm hurting, when I'm confused, when I'm trying to get through life? And as long as You are all I want, I know I will experience true joy.

In his classic devotional *My Utmost for His Highest,* the young preacher Oswald Chambers said,

Joy should not be confused with happiness. In fact, it is an insult to Jesus Christ to use the word happiness in connection with Him. The joy of Jesus was His absolute self-surrender and self-sacrifice to His Father—the joy of doing that which the Father sent Him to do...

Have the right relationship with God, finding your joy there, and out of you "will flow rivers of living water" (John 7:38).[9]

You and I are not our own. And we don't have a *right* to be happy. But we *do* have the privilege of experiencing His joy. And that joy comes when we surrender to our loving Master and say, "Whom have I in heaven but You? And there is none upon earth that I desire besides You."

STEP #6 *Toward Healing and Wholeness*

Relinquish your right to yourself.

*True surrender means recognizing your life is not your own;
you belong to a loving Master who has your best at heart.*

LET THE HEALING CONTINUE

1. Make a list of all you have felt you have a "right" to in your life (be honest, as this is a step of surrender to God):

2. Prayerfully, tell God about each of these items and surrender them to His will.

3. Read James 1:2-4 and write it out below as a reminder and an encouragement that when you surrender to Him, He brings joy.

4. To abide in Christ means to remain or continue with Him. What is one practical way you can abide in Him every day? (Below I have listed some suggestions for you, and you may want to add one or more of your own. Then commit yourself to following through.)

    *   I will set an appointment to spend time with God in prayer and reading His Word.

        My appointment time:
        My reading plan:

    *   I will take a walk with Him daily and pour out my heart to Him.

        Time of my walk:
        Place where I will walk:

    *   Every day at noon I will present to Him a verbal "five minutes of praise" for who He is and all He has done in my life.

    *   I will start my day with worship music and spend ten minutes in quiet reflection on His Word.

    *   _____
        _____

A Prayer of Hope and Healing

I thought it appropriate to end this chapter with a prayer from Jill Kelly's book *Prayers of Hope for the Brokenhearted*. Having learned that her life is not her own, she lives daily knowing that rather than having a right to be happy, God is reserving His right for her to be holy. He is waiting to do the same with you and me. Let's pray this one together:

Heavenly Father, my life is in Your hands.
Yesterday, today, and forever, I am safe and secure in You.
Lord, please help me to know that You are in control.
Help me to believe You are at work in my life right now,
even when I don't see it.
Help me to trust in what I do not see,
when what I see is so painful.
Please help me to know You are taking care of my needs.

You are faithful and good, trustworthy and present.
In You I find grace and forgiveness, healing and hope.
You have not left me alone in my trials.
You are with me right now, and You have promised to
never leave me nor forsake me.
Father, please help me to believe that Your plans for me and
my family are good.

Lord, thank You for listening to my cries for help.
Thank You for loving me so much.
Help me to believe You and the promises You have made.
Forgive me when I doubt You and Your love.
I believe, Lord. Forgive me for my unbelief.[10]

I'll Never Really Be Loved

Recognizing Real Versus Distorted Love

B ecky grew up longing for love just as most of us do. But unfortunately, she experienced the opposite.

Having been molested for several years as a child, she then found
herself in an abusive marriage with a man who cheated on her and
divorced her. Then when she thought she had finally found a true man
of God and given him four years of her life, she found out he was cheating on her with a woman from another church.

"Growing up being abused for many years has a tendency to make
one feel unloved, and being cheated on by my ex-husband and then
the other man made me feel very undesirable many times," Becky said.
"I think many women who have been cheated on come to the assump-
tion that if they had been good enough or pretty enough then their
husband wouldn't have cheated on them."

Becky, like so many women whose hearts have been broken, has
often asked herself and others, "What's wrong with me?"

But like so many of us do, Becky was asking the wrong question.

The question is not "What is wrong with me?" but rather, "What is
wrong with that representation of 'love'?"

It is ingrained in us, as women, to long for love and the happily-ever-after we've heard about since we were little girls. Just this
morning I received yet another email that asked questions many other
women have raised in their letters:

Where's the happiness, peace, and abundance in life? When am I going to see a simple and normal dream come true— like all other girls have—of having someone to love me, hold me, and protect me? If I'm praying to God and I'm still hurting, what's the point? Truly, is there a reason for me to hold on or to believe?

Our Longing for Love

Oh, the longings of a woman's heart to be loved! We learn from a young age that "love" is something that is wonderful to *feel*. And so we long for it. As we grow older, when someone notices us, is kind to us, or desires us physically, we interpret that as "love." And for a moment what we perceive as love may *feel* wonderful. Yet the moment that professed love is withheld, withdrawn completely, or used to manipulate us, it becomes the most painful thing we've ever experienced.

What is your story of careless, imperfect, or distorted love? Was it an abusive or absent father? Did you have a critical or emotionally distant mother? Did someone you love reject you? Did someone you trust betray you? I've heard countless stories of distorted love, lived through a few of them, and I am still standing here to tell you that I've seen clearly the other side—that place where you look back on your childhood or your early dating years or some hurtful memory and you realize that what you saw or experienced back then was distorted love, imperfect love, an impostor of the real thing.

And yet that place of discernment between distorted and real love— where broken hearts are finally healed—*does* exist. And I want to help you get there. I want to help you find that place where you too recognize that the wounds you experienced through distorted love were part of the battle you endured in order to eventually recognize and embrace pure and perfect love.

Unfortunately in this world, before we can understand perfect, self-less love, we sometimes have to see (or worse yet, experience) its opposite. Think about it. Has God graciously taught you, while growing up or in hindsight, what you *don't* want in your home, in your marriage, in your personal life? Did you learn what you really do want by seeing its opposite? What *not* to do. Who *not* to marry. How *not* to act or react.

Sharon, whose story is in chapter 2, grew up seeing the complete opposite of love. She saw a distorted, twisted, self-seeking "love" through the manipulative and abusive actions of her father. Being a young child, she had no frame of reference that would help her understand what love really is. Thus, this woman who experienced the worst of the worst had to relearn, as an adult, what love really is by looking at who God really is.

Carol's Story

Carol was also acquainted with distorted love. She grew up feeling unloved and unwanted. As the daughter of an angry, abusive alcoholic, her wounds increased as she learned the story of why her father started drinking heavily.

When Carol's mother was six months pregnant she got up at night to check on Carol, who was then a year old, and tripped over the family dog and fell, causing her to go into premature labor. Carol's baby brother was born and lived only one day. Both her parents were devastated by the loss. But little Carol was never told anything about it. She pieced together the story years later by talking to relatives and relying on what she remembered while growing up. She also learned that her father turned away from his faith in God after the death of her little brother because he had wanted a son so much. He had two daughters from a previous marriage, and then Carol was born. When his newborn son died, he snapped.

"I never felt loved by my father and was abandoned by him, both physically and emotionally," Carol said.

When Carol was an adult she left home and had a family of her own. But 11 years into her marriage, her alcoholic husband abandoned her and their two daughters when she confronted him about his drinking.

"I was abandoned by my father, and mother for a while, and then by my husband. *It must be me,* I thought."

She learned to get along as a single parent and saw God's provision, but lived for a long time with an emptiness in her heart that told her she was not desirable, and not good enough to keep a man's love.

Carol learned through hurtful experiences what love is not. And her first experience with real love was when she met Jesus and understood that His unconditional and sacrificial love for her was so amazingly different from anything she had experienced from her parents or husband.

"So many things happened in my younger years [to shape my view of love] that I had no control over, and then being married to an alcoholic who abandoned me was also heartbreaking. But all these things brought me closer and closer to the only One who matters—the One who loves me no matter what! He is my husband, my father, my brother, my friend. He is *everything* to me!"

Where We Go Wrong

Where a woman goes wrong is when her husband becomes everything to her. Or her boyfriend. Or her idea of what love must be. Frequently she will expect to be fulfilled from someone offering her love, and when that person ends up disappointing her, she finds herself devastated.

Naturally, when a woman marries, she expects it to be forever. She hears promises and a vow claiming "till death do us part" and she believes it. But oh the heartache when she discovers those promises broken and that vow has turned to a lie. It didn't last forever. His heart changed. Betrayal. Abandonment. Rejection. Hurt.

Sometimes we are the ones who end the marriage because our expectations of love were not met. So we keep looking for it in someone else. Until we realize the well is empty and we have come up dry.

Gina emailed me in response to a devotional I wrote about the inconsolable longings women feel and how God is the only One who satisfies. In her email she talked about learning the hard way that no love, marriage, or man on earth can ultimately satisfy:

> I am a three-times-married, three-times-divorced 63-year-old woman. The last time I was married for 23 years and have been divorced now for two years. All of my marriages left me

longing for companionship and understanding. Each husband, although different from the previous, was incapable of
giving me the nurturing and unconditional love I so craved
from childhood. But as you said in your devotional, people
will fail us—over and over—as we fail them.

I never found the satisfaction and filling in marriage
that I have found in my life now filled with God. He meets
my every need. As I steep myself in His love and His Word,
my heart is full. It seems ironic that had I had then what I
have now, I would probably still be married.

Gina's words, written in hindsight, offer us a valuable perspective.
When we long to receive from others the kind of love that only God is
capable of giving, we will continue to be disappointed in our earthly
relationships. Only God can offer the living water that our souls long
for and the perfect love our hearts were created to absorb.

God created marriage to illustrate to us the kind of love and intimacy He wants to share with His people. He told His people in Isaiah
54:5, "Your Maker is your husband, the LORD of hosts is His name."
God has been a perfect husband to us, providing for us, nurturing us,
protecting us, and faithfully loving and forgiving us time after time.
And He wants to experience from us the response of a faithful wife—a
trust, singularity of commitment, and faithfulness that lasts for eternity.

God, throughout the Old Testament, accused His people of adultery when they pursued and worshipped false, foreign gods. And in the
New Testament, He called those who are trusting His Son for their forgiveness and eternal life His "bride," and He will one day share with us
a wedding feast (Revelation 19:9). The examples are all over Scripture.
God has pursued us like a bridegroom pursues his beloved bride. And
He has demonstrated to us what unconditional, sacrificial love looks
like that marriages here on earth should be expressing and experiencing.

God even prepared a happily-ever-after for us to experience with
Him someday (John 14:3). But the problem is that, in our humanity,
in our longing for something temporal that feels good, we tend to look
for love in all the wrong places. Chances are *you*, at one time, believed

you found it in someone else. And then you were disappointed as you realized that love was capable of disappointing you, hurting you, and even betraying you.

I'm certainly not blaming you, my friend. I've done the same thing. I've looked to others to fill me completely, to show me pure, unconditional, godly love and to bind up my hurts and heal my insecurities. But no one this side of heaven is able to love us perfectly, nor are we able to love others in that way. That is because we (and those we look to for love) still live in our fleshly (and often selfish) bodies. Because we still give in to our selfish natures. Because we still lack the spiritual perfection we will not receive until we are with Jesus.

As long as we're drawing what we need from another person, we are drawing from a well that will never satisfy, and we will keep coming up thirsty and longing for more. We will find ourselves empty, dry, parched. Only when we surrender that hole in our heart to Jesus will it finally be filled.[1]

Filling the Vacancy

Jan, a women's ministry director in Arkansas, recently shared with the women at her church her story of trying to fill the vacancy in her heart with something other than God. By the time she was born, her parents were already divorced, leaving Jan longing for a father to love and care for her. At the age of five her dream for a father came true as her mother remarried and Jan was legally adopted by the new man in her life. She was excited and her expectations were high. But instead of being nurtured and loved the way she envisioned, she experienced fear, disappointment, and more rejection through emotional abuse and neglect on the part of both of her parents.

With a continued vacancy in her heart for a daddy to love her, Jan began to invite other things into her life to fill that vacancy. She ended up falling in love with a man and sought his attention to fill the hole in her heart. But he was just a man. He couldn't fill her completely. His love wouldn't make up for the feelings of rejection that still plagued her. Jan eventually looked outside her marriage to fill the emptiness that remained in her heart. As a result, she ultimately found herself rejected by two fathers and facing the rejection of her husband on account of her unfaithfulness to him and their marriage vows. It was then that she turned to God as the Father she never knew.

"He was the only One at that point in my life who I knew could save me," she said.

Jan knows today that God is her Father who has saved her, redeemed her, and adopted her as His child. "He has restored my marriage and shown me His unconditional love and forgiveness through my husband, children, and friends.

"God has filled the vacancies of my heart. He had long wanted to walk into those empty places in my heart and was waiting for me to surrender myself to Him."

Every one of us who experiences rejection of one sort or another looks to something else to fill that void, until we realize it can only be filled by the Lord Jesus. What have you filled the hole with? Only perfect love will close up the gaps.

A Picture of Perfect Love

If you've been wounded by what you *thought* was love, let's take a moment to discover what love *really* is.

First Corinthians 13:4-8 provides the Bible's most detailed description of love. It is read at weddings, quoted in cards, and held up as God's ideal instruction for us on how to love each other:

> Love is patient and kind. Love is not jealous or boastful or proud or rude. Love does not demand its own way. Love is not irritable, and it keeps no record of when it has been wronged. It is never glad about injustice but rejoices whenever the truth wins out. Love never gives up, never loses faith, is always hopeful, and endures through every circumstance...
> Love will last forever!" (NLT).

Although that passage serves as instruction and a goal for us on how to love others, it is interesting that it describes perfectly God's love toward us. So think about it: We are to love others as we are loved by

God. None of us can get it absolutely right, though. So how can we expect another human being to get it right all the time toward us? If we were to focus on how God loves us, we would recognize the impostors when they arrive. We would have more realistic expectations of others and, I believe, we would guard our hearts a little more closely.

So how do you focus on God's perfect love?

Refocusing on Real Love

In a letter to the first-century church at Ephesus, Jesus talked about pure and perfect love. He started out by listing all that this church had done in His name:

> I know your works, your labor, your patience, and that you cannot bear those who are evil. And you have tested those who say they are apostles and are not, and have found them liars; and you have persevered and have patience, and have labored for My name's sake and have not become weary (Revelation 2:2-3).

That's a pretty impressive résumé, isn't it? In fact, if you and I did all that this church was commended for, we might feel like really good followers of Christ. We might feel like we had His favor. We would feel, at the very least, like good, God-fearing, moral people.

That's why it's so surprising to see what Jesus said next: "*Yet I hold this against you*: You have forsaken the love you had at first" (verse 4 NIV, emphasis added).

In spite of all the good things the Ephesians were doing, God had a problem with them. They had lost their fervor and passion for Him. They had grown out of love.

In the New King James Version, this verse says, "You have left your first love."

We "leave" our first love when we express more passionate love for something or someone else, when we give that passion away to someone less deserving, or when we obey and serve God out of duty rather than devotion. When God isn't our first love, it's all downhill for us. Jesus went so far as to call attention to how far the Ephesians had fallen:

"Consider how far you have fallen! Repent and do the things you did at first."[2]

Jesus demands and deserves to be the first love in our lives. Throughout the Old Testament, God says He is a jealous God—not in a self-seeking way, but because He is deserving of our heart's devotion (Exodus 34:14). He paid the ultimate price for us. He simply won't tolerate being second or third or tenth in our lives. That is why Jesus urged the Ephesians to bring back the passion, to pursue Him again, to make Him their first love again. Let's see what we can learn from His exhortations:

1. Remember the height from which you've fallen

Do you recall a time in your life when you were a lot closer to God than you are right now? Do you long to have that passion back? Think about the first time you fell in love. Do you recall how that man had you heartsick? You were nearly obsessed with the thought of him. Hopefully you can recall a time when you first came to know Christ as well—when you first learned of His sacrifice for you and how that impacted your heart. God wants you to remember where you once were with Him. He wants you to regain the passion you once had for Him. You must recognize where you used to be in order to get back there again.

2. Repent (for seeking other loves above Him)

Who or what is it that eventually became more important to you than Christ? Even your hurts can become more important and closer to your heart than the Healer of your hurts. Tell God who or what it is that has replaced Him on the throne of your heart and how sorry you are that you allowed it to happen. Then commit yourself to never letting that object or person replace Him again. (The original Greek word for "repent" in Revelation 2:5 literally means to "think differently" or "reconsider."[3])

3. Return to the passion of the relationship

Jesus instructed those who had grown complacent to Him to "do the things you did at first" (verse 5 NIV). Did you at one time spend more time in His Word, more focused time in prayer, more time conversing with Him throughout your day? Did you at one time praise Him a lot more than you do now? Were you bragging on Him to others or letting everyone else know you'd found a new life in Him? Those are the things He wants you to do again—to reaffirm to yourself and others that He is the foremost love in your heart. Once you remember where you once were in the relationship, and you repent for having slipped away, you must then follow through by returning to that place and doing the things you once did. *Show* Him the love.

Guard Your Heart

I know it's easy to replace God with other things, to let something else slip onto the throne of our lives. When I was talking to Christina (whose story of growing up while running from the law is told in chapter 3) about the impact the Lord has made in her life, she gave me a silly yet convicting illustration of how easy it is for us to let something else, even something trivial, slide into God's spot on the throne of our lives.

"I heard my thoughts the other day," Christina told me. "I had that thought of 'Lord, my heart just skipped a beat over shoes. That is not where You would have my heart. You would have my heart only skip a beat for the things of You.'"

I'm ashamed to say that my heart, too, has skipped a beat over shoes (and those of you who know me personally can attest to that!). But as Christina said, that is not where God would have my heart. He doesn't want shoes or plans or dreams or desires or *any living thing* to have the throne of my heart. It is His. And He is the only One who can fill it completely.

I am not saying that we should not enjoy or appreciate pretty things or even that we should shun material objects. After all, I have multiple watches, handbags, and…yes…shoes! But I must work to keep myself in check, as Christina mentioned, to constantly monitor my heart and ask, "What is most important to me today?" Is it what I own? What I look like? What I'm wearing? Or is it who I know? And I want that thrill in my heart to come from my connection with God, that "I've gotta have it" to be over a closer relationship with Him, not something that I think will satisfy a temporary urge.

It's also possible to end up letting your heart skip a beat over people—a new man in your life, someone you met at work, or even a new baby or grandbaby. But Jesus clearly pointed out in His Word that "He who loves father or mother more than Me is not worthy of Me. And he who loves son or daughter more than Me is not worthy of Me" (Matthew 10:37). Those are tough words, but they come from a God who bought us with a price, who created us for His pleasure, and who commands us to love Him with all (not just part) of our heart, soul, mind, and strength.

Who or what is causing your heart to skip a beat right now? Who or what is occupying God's position on the throne of your heart? By asking that question you can come clean from the problem of looking to anything or anyone other than Him for your satisfaction. And you can spare yourself much hurt in the days to come. When something else becomes your first love, hurt is inevitable. However, when Christ is first in your life, you will recognize perfect love. And you won't be fooled by the substitutes any longer. You will hold your standard higher, you won't let your heart be misled again, and you will experience what it's like to *really* be loved. Guard your heart carefully, my sister. It belongs to Him alone.

STEP #7 *Toward Healing and Wholeness*

Recognize the difference between real and distorted love.
And embrace God's love as the only love that will satisfy.

LET THE HEALING CONTINUE

1. How have you identified love thus far in your life?

2. Can you look at your heartaches and see in them distorted love—the opposite of what God intended perfect love to look like? How so?

3. Read through the following verses and write a prayerful response next to each one, telling God how you feel about the way His Word describes His love for you:

    Isaiah 49:15-16—

    Jeremiah 31:3—

    Romans 8:37-39—

A Prayer for Returning to Your First Love

Lover of My Soul,

You have modeled unconditional, sacrificial love to me by giving up Your life for me so I can live with You eternally. What amazing love! There is nothing like it here on earth.

Lord, soothe the wounds in my heart that have developed over the course of my life because of my exposure to imperfect and distorted love. Take the salve of Your pure and perfect love and pour it over the rough edges of my heart and treat the wounds that still lie open from a broken, damaged heart.

Forgive me for seeking satisfaction from anyone or anything other than You. Take Your rightful place on the throne of my heart and keep it for You alone. Help me to guard my heart—and if I ever let anyone else begin to fill the space You have occupied, gently remind me that You are the only One who satisfies, and You will be second to no one.

My heart is Yours, Lord Jesus. Thank You for loving me like no one on earth has been able to. Thank You that Your love and affection for me is beyond comparison. And thank You that because of Your death and resurrection for me, my heart is now spoken for.

PART III:

Unveiling a New Heart

*I will give you a new heart and
put a new spirit in you;
I will remove from you your heart of
stone and give you a heart of flesh.*

<small>Ezekiel 36:26 niv</small>

I Can Finally Be Free
Releasing Yourself Through Forgiveness

I f you knew Deanna's story, you might think she had every right to be resentful toward every person she's ever trusted.

But Deanna knows the freedom that comes through forgiveness, especially when it's hard to give.

Deanna grew up with an emotionally distant father and a critical mother whom Deanna felt loved her conditionally, based on how she performed.

But after spending all her childhood years trying to please and earn her parents' love, she came to learn she was adopted.

"That made things worse. I wondered what was wrong with me that my birth parents gave me up. And it hurt that my adoptive parents felt they had to keep this information a secret for so long," Deanna said.

The wounds in Deanna's heart compounded even more the day she learned that her husband had been having an affair with her best friend.

Abandonment. Feelings of rejection. The pain of emotional distance. Secrets. Lies. And now, the ultimate betrayal from not only her husband, but her best friend as well.

Deanna remembers being immobilized by sadness, feeling like a walking ghost at times. Everywhere she went she was physically present, but not emotionally present. "I carried my wounds for so long, I no longer saw them. I hid my hurts rather than deal with them. Shame was a cloak I wore at all times."

The Day She Died Inside

Deanna and Brian were married almost six years when she learned about Brian's affair. Deanna found out after they had moved to another state and the husband of her best friend called her with the news. When Deanna called her friend about it, her friend denied responsibility and shifted the blame for the affair on Deanna.

"When my husband came home, he told me all the details of what happened and what didn't happen and then pretty much told me he didn't want to talk about it anymore. He also told me that I had grounds for divorce if I chose to divorce him," Deanna said.

Deanna intended to divorce Brian, but as she was thinking through what she would do and where she would go, she learned she was pregnant with their first child. (They had no children previously and didn't intend to have any.) Deanna didn't want to be a single parent, so she chose to stay in the marriage for the sake of her child. But she continued to be miserable, living with a man whom she couldn't trust anymore. She found herself going through the motions in her marriage. Two years after her daughter was born, they had another child.

Although Brian was repentant and desired reconciliation, Deanna was still numb from all the pain in her life and didn't care about her marriage anymore. Resentment and bitterness had built a thick barrier to any soft spot in her heart.

"We continued to attend church and felt the Holy Spirit working in each of our lives, but we never talked about the affair. I still had unanswered questions that I couldn't ask. I guess I compartmentalized all of this instead of dealing with it. A pastor approached us and asked us to lead a small group study about marriage. My husband agreed and it about killed me. We were to lead this group when we ourselves had unfinished business to take care of. I had detached myself from Brian and didn't want to grow closer to this man who had one foot in the door of our marriage and the other outside checking to see if the goods were better!

"About this time, Brian was getting serious about his walk with Christ and wanted to be open with me. He told me how he lusted after other women whom he worked with. I had heard enough and I was ready to walk. He was trying to be transparent, but I was not ready to hear that he had a wandering heart and mind. I built this wall around my heart and soul and would not let him in. We were basically roommates at this point. I didn't want to share anything with him because I feared he would be able to use it against me and hurt me. I didn't trust him anymore. I did not think he had our family's best interest at heart. We were detached and had nothing in common. I was ready to walk, but we had these two children to raise."

Then Brian suggested the two of them attend a class at their church called "Divorce-proofing Your Marriage." She went reluctantly and then the two of them were invited to attend an Emergency Marriage Seminar,[1] which was open to only a few couples. "This is what saved our marriage," Deanna said. "It was not until this time that I could safely ask my questions about the affair and tell my husband how it made me feel. This was the start of our healing process."

After the Emergency Marriage Seminar, Brian started attending a Bible study for men who struggled with being emotionally or sexually faithful to their wives. As of this writing, he has attended every week for the last four years. He has an accountability partner and has gone through all the steps required to earn back his wife's trust. And Deanna became involved in a small group with other women who are recovering from similar hurts and she is moving forward in her process of learning to trust her husband again.

"There was no quick fix," Deanna said. "We are still working through issues, and I am still learning to trust my husband. I don't fully trust him and he knows it. He knows he will have to earn back my trust and that could take a year or 25 years. Yet even though we are still working on trust, I love him dearly and wouldn't trade him for the world."

How did Deanna's love for Brian come back? How was she able to renew her hope in spite of her past hurts? How was she able to remove that cloak of shame and begin wearing her new identity in Christ?

"Forgiveness is the key," she said. "Forgiveness is not taking someone else off the hook; it is setting yourself free. When you forgive, you realize you were the one on the hook or in bondage, and you must forgive to move on.

"Forgiveness is a process and is not always easy, but to not forgive is to saddle yourself with some heavy baggage you don't need to carry around!"

At one time Deanna felt she could never forgive her husband or anyone else who had caused her hurt. "But when I *did* forgive, I found out that *I* was the one being held captive by not forgiving."

Our Route to Freedom

Like Deanna, we may sometimes refuse to forgive our offenders because we don't want to let them off the hook, because they haven't earned our forgiveness, or because we don't trust them. But because forgiveness is the key to moving forward from our hurts, let's look at what it really means to forgive someone. We can do this by debunking the most common misconceptions about forgiveness and stacking them up against what God's Word has to say about the subject.

Misconception #1—Forgiveness Must Be Earned by Our Offender

We often believe those who have hurt us must apologize, express their remorse, and ask for our forgiveness in order to be forgiven. Or we expect them to somehow make up for the hurt they have caused us. In Deanna's case, there was nothing Brian could do to make up for the hurt he had caused her. The damage had been done. Yet we are commanded to forgive whether the other person asks for it or not. Whether the other person is remorseful or not. Whether the other person deserves it or not.

Deanna said, "It is very hard to forgive and it is unnatural, but we are commanded to forgive others just as Christ forgave us."

If you are waiting for your offender to apologize or admit his or her wrongdoing, the truth is, it may never happen. And if the person who abused you, abandoned you, or betrayed you really did feel remorseful, would it be enough to take the pain away? No. So your forgiveness cannot be dependent upon your offender's attitude or actions. The fact that they wounded you badly in the first place may be an indication that they are incapable of mending that wound for you. That's why forgiveness is extended by *you*, willingly, as an act of obedience to God and an unwavering trust in His ability to work it out so you can move forward out of the pain and into the purposes God has for you.

When Jesus went to the cross for you, He forgave your sins *before* you ever asked for His forgiveness (Romans 5:8). He wants you to model that same grace and forgiveness to others, regardless of the measure of pain they have inflicted upon you (Colossians 3:12-13).

Sharon, whose story is told in chapter 2, never received an apology from her abusive father. Up until the time he died, he continued his cruel, emotional manipulation toward her. If Sharon were to wait until the day he deserved forgiveness, that day would never come. If she were to wait for an apology or some sign of remorse from him, that day will never come either. But Sharon has released his hold on her by releasing him and his offenses to God. She no longer bears resentment in her heart and mind. She knows only grace that she extends toward others because of the grace God has shown toward her.

So don't wait for the other person to take the first step. That day might never come. But the day has come for you to *choose* to offer forgiveness willingly.

Misconception #2—Forgiveness Is a One-time Act

We would also like to believe that when we forgive someone we only have to do it once and then we can be done with it—we don't have to think about it anymore. That would be nice if it worked that way. But our hurts often don't heal overnight. (Remember that Deanna's healing process took a lot longer because she wasn't allowed to ask Brian questions about his affair.) We are often reminded of our hurts when memories pop up now and then or if we have to face the consequences of them daily. Even if you genuinely forgive someone one day, old feelings of resentment could come to the surface when you least expect it. That's why forgiveness is a continual decision.

When Jesus' disciple, Peter, asked Jesus if he should forgive a brother who sins against him up to seven times, Peter must have thought he was being generous. After all, if someone offends you once, you forgive them. If they do it twice, then you're being gracious to forgive them. But I'm sure you're familiar with the saying, "Fool me once, shame on you; fool me twice, shame on *me*." Who in their right mind would forgive the same person up to *seven* times? But Jesus instructed Peter to forgive that same brother "up to seventy times seven" (Matthew 18:22). Jesus was reinforcing to Peter that his forgiveness should be without limits, just as God's forgiveness toward us is without limits.

It's interesting that Peter didn't ask Jesus how many times he should forgive *all the people* who had hurt him during his lifetime. The question was about how many times he should continue to forgive *the same person*. And let's face it, those who are the most difficult to forgive are those who offend us repeatedly. Yet, Jesus wanted Peter—and us—to understand that forgiveness is something we do continually, even when it involves the same person over and over again. You may have forgiven a person for something years ago, but when feelings of resentment or traces of hurt from long ago come to the surface again, you are to continue to forgive. Just because you have forgiven a person once does not mean that's the end of it. Every time the offense comes to mind, forgive that person again. Forgiveness is continual.

Misconception #3—To Forgive Means to Forget

Scripture tells us that when God forgives our sin, He *forgets* it as well:

- "I, even I, am He who blots out your transgressions for My own sake; and I will not remember your sins" (Isaiah 43:25).

- "As far as the east is from the west, so far has He removed our transgressions from us" (Psalm 103:12).

- "You will again have compassion on us; you will tread our sins underfoot and hurl all our iniquities into the depths of the sea" (Micah 7:19 NIV).

Wouldn't it be great if our minds worked liked God's? I wish we had the ability to forget our sins, as well as the sins of others. But we, in our humanity, have a difficult time forgetting the things that have hurt us most. If a spouse has left and you are dealing with the ongoing, daily consequences of his decision to abandon his family, you will not be able to *forget* what he has done. If you were injured by another person and you still bear physical scars from that abuse, you will still *remember* what happened every time you see those scars. But just because you *remember* an offense doesn't mean you haven't *forgiven* it. It just means you aren't able to forget in the way God does.

Each time you remember the offense that you have forgiven, follow through with these steps of forgiveness:

1. Admit that you were wronged.
2. Acknowledge that your offender owes you for his transgression.
3. Release your offender of his debt to you.

As I mentioned earlier, you may need to do this every time the offense comes to your mind. But don't beat yourself up for still remembering. There's a difference between merely remembering something and *dwelling* on it. To remember it is natural. To dwell on it is unhealthy.

Deanna said that when her mind begins to bring back offenses from the past, she practices 2 Corinthians 10:5, which tells us to "demolish arguments and every pretension that sets itself up against the knowledge of God" and to "take captive every thought to make it obedient to Christ" (NIV).

"I constantly have to take my thoughts captive and not let them accuse me or anyone else," she said.

Misconception #4—Forgiveness Means Restoration or Reunion

Mira was frustrated with her college roommate, "Jody." Because of some unresolved financial issues, and the fact that Jody lied to Mira on a number of occasions, they didn't talk for several months. When Jody found Mira on Facebook recently, she finally apologized for what she had done, but Mira was reluctant to restore the relationship. It was then that she was counseled that to forgive someone doesn't mean you have to trust that person again. It doesn't even mean you have to restore the relationship. Rather, to forgive means you no longer expect that person to "repay" you for the hurt brought against you. Mira experienced freedom when she realized she could extend kindness yet could also maintain safe boundaries. She didn't have to put herself in a position where she would be lied to, taken advantage of, or cheated on again.

Through the years, I have counseled many women who were in emotionally and physically abusive relationships and reinforced to them that forgiving their offender does not mean giving him another chance to hurt them. It does not mean reconciling the relationship if true repentance on the other person's part is not involved. It does not mean trusting that person again if that person has not earned their trust. A person who has harmed you does not have to earn your forgiveness, but he definitely has to earn your trust if he has betrayed it. You can release a person from his offense and yet keep protective boundaries around your heart, mind, and body. God commands that we forgive, and that we do so freely. But to reunite with a cheating and unrepentant spouse, a friend who has slandered you, or a boss who has mistreated you is an entirely different matter. You can forgive that person, but you don't have to have a *relationship* with him or her again.

Sometimes we think that if we do forgive someone else, the relationship will be restored in a good way. That is often not the case.

Stephanie's father left her mother and abandoned the family when she was about five years old. Then after he remarried and became a stepparent to his second wife's children, Stephanie's father started arranging for her and her sister to have weekend visits with him.

"All growing up, it was a rough relationship. I was mad at him, and he constantly put both my sister and me second to his new wife and children. From what I can remember, our conversations were always hostile. I was very angry at him. After I talked to him on the phone, I would cry or be really upset. I let myself be hurt by his empty promises to see me more or call more often to stay in touch.

"It wasn't until I became a Christian that I realized I needed to forgive my dad. I wrote him a letter and said I was finally putting all this behind me. I forgave him for walking out on our family and told him I would like to have a closer relationship with him. He called and said he was shocked that I had held on to the pain of the divorce for so long. He thought I had let that go a long time ago. I was totally shocked to hear him say that! I mean, what did he make of all the conversations during which I would become upset? Apparently he hadn't noticed, and hadn't given it that much thought. I'll probably never know, and that's okay. As soon as that conversation passed I felt better.

"He still makes the same empty promises and says hurtful things, but ever since I've forgiven him, God has given me peace. I was hoping for a healed relationship, but that hasn't happened, and it doesn't affect me as much as it used to. It still hurts, but I'm able to let it go and walk away calm. I'm at as much peace as one can be with the fact that I will always come as an afterthought with my dad."

When you forgive, it doesn't mean your relationship with your offender will be fully restored. It just means that you will have peace for having extended forgiveness and you will be able to move forward with life.

The Benefits of Forgiveness

Now that we've cleared up some of the misconceptions about forgiveness, let's look at the beautiful benefits of offering to another the forgiveness God has offered you.

Forgiveness Frees You to Be Obedient to God

Jesus tells us to forgive as we have been forgiven.

Every one of us has offended, betrayed, or hurt God in some way or another. Yet He has freely and generously forgiven us. The debt of gratitude we owe Him is paid out as we freely and generously forgive others.

In Matthew 18:23-35, Jesus told a parable about a king who wanted to settle accounts with his servants. As he began the settlement, a man who owed him the equivalent of millions of dollars was brought to him. Since he was not able to repay the king, the king ordered that he and his wife and his children and all that he had be sold to repay the debt. But, the servant fell on his knees and begged the king to be patient with him, and he would pay back everything. The king took pity on the man, canceled his entire debt, and let him go.

After that servant left, he found one of his fellow servants who owed him a few dollars and grabbed his neck, began choking him, and demanded that he pay up. That man fell to his knees and begged his creditor with the same words his creditor had just earlier said to the king: "Have patience with me, and I will pay you all" (verse 29). But the first servant refused, and had the second servant thrown into prison until he could repay the few dollars.

When the king heard about what had happened, he called the first servant back and said, "You wicked servant! I forgave you all that debt because you begged me. Should you not also have had compassion on your fellow servant, just as I had pity on you?" In anger, the king turned him over to be tortured until he paid back all he owed. Jesus summed up that story with a warning about the consequences of not forgiving others after we have been so graciously forgiven by God: "This is how my heavenly Father will treat each of you unless you forgive your brother or sister from your heart" (Matthew 18:35 NIV).

"I could never forgive her for what she did to me" said a high school–aged girl in reference to a former best friend who gossiped about her and then "stole" her boyfriend. "But Maribel," I responded, "do you realize that God forgave you for something that deserved death? And if you accept His forgiveness for every wrong you have committed, you are expected and obligated to forgive anyone who has ever hurt you, as well?"[2] She didn't like the sound of that. But it made her think twice about her hardened heart toward the girl she said she'd never forgive.

Forgiveness Frees You to Live Out God's Purpose for Your Life

Because Deanna was able to forgive her husband, Brian, the two of them are now ministering to other couples in their small group at church. But if she had said, "That's it—no more! I'm finished with this marriage," what might she have held back from God, who was waiting to redeem and restore the situation?

In chapter 1, we looked briefly at the biblical account of Joseph, who was hated by his jealous brothers and sold into slavery. He was then unjustly imprisoned and eventually released and raised up to govern all of Egypt, second in command only to Pharaoh himself. God worked through the evil intentions of Joseph's brothers to work something extraordinary in his life. Let's look again at what happened when Joseph came face-to-face with his evil brothers a couple decades later.

After Joseph came to power in Egypt, the famine he told his brothers about in a dream years earlier came to pass. His brothers, famished and impoverished, came to Egypt for food. Through a series of events, they came to meet—they didn't recognize Joseph, but he recognized them. Instead of a "get even" confrontation (Joseph had the authority to have them immediately executed!), he revealed himself to them and then cried with them tears of forgiveness and relief.

How could Joseph do such a thing? He believed what they had done was all part of God's divine plan for his life. He was so certain of God's goodness and purposes that he was able to release his offenders as mere pawns in the palm and plan of a sovereign God.

Years later, when Joseph's father died, his brothers believed he might finally execute judgment on them. But Joseph's gentle response was, "Do not be afraid, for am I in God's place? As for you, you meant evil against me, but God meant it for good in order to bring about this present result, to preserve many people alive."[3]

Can *you* look at all that has happened in *your* life and acknowledge that God can take all the hurt, rejection, and evil you've experienced and work it for good? If you can, I guarantee you that praise for God will replace any pity you had for yourself or any plans you had for revenge.

It's absolutely essential for us to recognize God's sovereign control over our lives. That's what enables us to say, "I don't hold that person responsible and I don't resent him, because God was ultimately in control of my life." That is surrender. That is maturity. That is forgiveness.

In his book *Say Goodbye to Regret*, Robert Jeffress points out that

> Joseph was able to see the hand of God in every hurt he had experienced. Yes, his brothers had wronged him; but Joseph believed in a God who was bigger than his brothers. Joseph believed that God was able to take the wrong actions and evil motivations of his brothers and use them for his good and for God's eternal plan. A firm belief in the

sovereignty of God was a strong motivation for Joseph's willingness to forgive.[4]

And Jeffress believes it wasn't Joseph's only motivation.

Forgiveness Frees You from Emotional Bondage

Jeffress believes "Joseph also had a selfish reason for releasing his brothers of their obligation: he was tired of serving as a prisoner of regret." He continues:

> Years earlier [Joseph] had been imprisoned by the unjust accusation of Potiphar's wife, and God had miraculously freed him. But even though he had ascended to the highest position in Pharaoh's court, Joseph was still an emotional prisoner of his brothers' mistreatment so many years ago.[5]

Genesis 45:1-2 tells us of the emotional reaction Joseph had when he finally revealed his identity to his brothers. Look at the pent-up emotions that finally erupted:

> Then Joseph could not control himself before all those who stood by him, and he cried, "Have everyone go out from me." So there was no man with him when Joseph made himself known to his brothers. He wept so loudly that the Egyptians heard it, and the household of Pharaoh heard of it.

Jeffress says, "Joseph could not stand the pain any longer. He needed to unshackle himself from the emotional chains of past wrongs that enslaved him. And forgiveness was the only key that would work."[6]

Stephanie, who was finally able to forgive her dad for leaving her family, says, "It really is true that forgiveness is not for the other person as much as it is for us. Being angry with my dad only hurt me. He had no clue the effect he had on me, and still doesn't."

Are you still in chains to the person who has hurt you? Would you like to be free from the bitterness that is binding you and preventing you from moving forward in your life?

Take some time right now to admit to God that you have been hurt.

Go ahead and acknowledge to the Lord that the person who hurt you owes you for what they have done to you. Then confess any desires for revenge you may have felt, and pray along these lines: "Lord, I choose to forgive ___(name of person)___ for ___(list what the person did that hurt you)___, even though it made me feel ___(painful memories or feelings)___."[7]

Whether your offender is sorry or not, whether he ever expresses remorse or not, your decision to release him of his offense and debt to you will release *you* from your prison of bitterness and enable you to move onward.

Freedom to Move Forward

Once you forgive those who have offended you, your eyes will be opened to see the many blessings God has placed in front of you as He's been healing your heart.

That's what happened with Jami. A mother of two children who thought she was the last wife in the world who would suffer from a cheating husband, Jami experienced multiple incidents of betrayal and abandonment. But she found that as she forgave James she was able to focus on all God was doing in her life and the lives of her children. And she was able to move forward.

"Forgiveness hasn't come easy for me," she said. "It is still a process between me and God, especially on the days that James promises to do something with our girls and doesn't show up; when he misses their proms, homecomings, birthdays and other special events. God teaches me to surrender it all to Him. It is not my burden to carry.

"God has provided for us, protected us, loved us and blessed us in so many ways. One day my youngest daughter hugged me and said, 'There is no other place that I want to live because here with you is the best.' I started to cry. Our house knows peace, love, and laughter today and I truly believe it is because God is our unshakeable foundation.

"The other day I asked God, 'What happens to a person who deserts his family and lives for himself?' I clearly heard God say to me, 'The better question to ask is, "What blessings are bestowed on the person who stays and provides for and protects that little family?"'"

Jami said, "The Lord knows what I've been through. He has

protected, provided for, and loved us unconditionally over the last five years. He has met *all* of my needs and more. He has built my character, increased my patience, and made me more persistent."

Like Jami, you may be thinking, *But what about that person who did me wrong?* Yet God wants you focused on what He's doing in your life and the blessings He is bringing about because of your heart of obedience and your willingness to forgive.

Look at the blessings He's given you. You are forgiven. And now that you too can forgive, you are truly free.

STEP #8 *Toward Healing and Wholeness*

Release your offender—and yourself—through forgiveness.

Freedom comes through letting the other person off of your emotional hook.

LET THE HEALING CONTINUE

Now it's time to practice the principles laid out in this chapter.

1. As you sit quietly before God, ask Him to make you aware of any residue of bitterness that exists in you over someone who has hurt you. If someone comes to mind, that is the Spirit of God letting you know of someone you still need to forgive. Lay that person and the offense on the altar of your heart and pray the following prayer: "Lord, I choose to forgive _____ for _____, even though it made me feel _____."

    Do this as many times as it takes with as many people as you need to. God is listening. And He is waiting to release you from the chains that have held you hostage to this hurt.

2. Read the following passages of Scripture and write out the verses so

you are more likely to remember them. Circle the ones you need to commit to memory.

Psalm 103:12—

Isaiah 1:18—

Jeremiah 31:34—

Micah 7:19—

Ephesians 1:7—

Colossians 3:13—

1 John 1:9—

3. Now spend the next several minutes thanking God for the forgiveness He has extended to you and the ability He has given you to forgive others.

A Prayer of Freedom

Thank You, Lord Jesus, for the incredible freedom that You give when I lay before You my wounds and surrender to You my offenses and choose to forgive those who have offended me. Lord, thank You that You are good, loving, and just. You will not only take care of the situations that are out of my hands, but You will let me walk in peace and security and freedom when I surrender to You the situations and people I can't control.

In order to please Your heart, and for You alone, I choose to live a life of forgiveness. I praise You as Your people did long ago when they said,

Our God, no one is like you.

We are all that is left of your chosen people,

And you freely forgive our sin and guilt.

You don't stay angry forever;

You're glad to have pity and pleased to be merciful.

You will trample on our sins and throw them into the sea.

You will keep your word and be faithful to

Jacob and to Abraham,

As you promised our ancestors many years ago

(Micah 7:18-20 CEV).

I Can Experience Joy Again
Refreshing Your Soul Through Praise

C yndi has experienced loss all her life.
She has endured the loss of her health, the loss of her identity through her husband's career change and relocation, the loss of her ability to have children, and the loss of loved ones in traumas and tragedies.

"Loss continues...loss will always continue," Cyndi said.

But she is not bitter. She is not fearful or hesitant about life. She is not a shell of a woman who bears the battle scars of much hurt. She is, to the contrary, a joyful, optimistic woman who constantly encourages others. That's because she learned, after much hurt, to praise God in the midst of pain.

But Cyndi wasn't always that way. For the first 20 or so years of her life she was simply trying to survive.

"I was the youngest of 13 grandchildren, their ages ranging from 5 through 18. I watched many people in my family get sick and die," she said. "I was constantly watching grief, sickness, separation, and tragedy."

When Cyndi was 12, she lost both her grandmothers to long-term illnesses during a ten-week span of time. "As long as I can remember, they had been sick and in critical condition."

Later in her young adult years, her grandfather, with whom she was very close, was thrown from a tractor. The tractor ran over him, and his neck was broken. He was airlifted, unrecognizable, to a hospital as Cyndi watched the tragic scene.

"My dad's tragic loss of a younger brother, his father's horrible death, and then my dad's receiving a diagnosis of heart disease and later prostate cancer seemed too much to bear for one man and one family. The same year that my uncle was killed in a tragic boating accident, I lost three high school friends right before graduation—in car accidents and a drowning.

"So many things happened in our lives, but we just moved on. I was always the singer at the funerals. I learned how to hold it all together and sing."

But it wasn't until Cyndi was in a hospital bed years later that she finally chose to *live*—not just survive losses in life. When she came face-to-face with the possibility of dying from an eating disorder, Cyndi chose life—the kind that Jesus came to bring. Jesus said in John 10:10: "The thief comes only to steal and kill and destroy; I came that they may have life, and have it abundantly" (NASB).

The thieves that wanted to destroy Cyndi were death, grief, fear, addiction, and a desire to control her circumstances. But the One who came to bring her life convinced her that if she gave Him the throne in her life, she would experience joy.

Instead of continuing to just "hold it together," Cyndi wanted to experience that joy.

And she did as she got to know this God who had allowed the suffering she had seen and found that He truly is good, loving, and capable of being the source of her joy.

When Cyndi surrendered to God and began putting Him first in her life, the pain didn't stop. But her attitude toward it changed.

After discovering helpful insights about herself through Christian counseling, and finally accepting God's grace and power to help her recover from an eating disorder, she went on to graduate, teach music, and marry her husband, Keith. Since then, she said she has endured "much turmoil with Keith's injury, our future, the added stress of the practice, large home chores to handle, loss of a dream with some land we owned, financial stress, my illness with meningitis, two hurricanes to go through and recover from, and all the unknowns for about eight years.

"Those types of losses have shaped me and given me a lot of perspective on how God works and why," Cyndi said. "I don't question God when these kinds of things happen to me."

Instead of questioning God, she praises Him in the midst of her pain. "Every trial is an exercise of strength and preparation for the next step in my life. They are like building blocks of faith on which I can stand and find rest.

"God's faithfulness in my seasons of adversity turned me into a true worshiper more than any pleasant season of my life," she said.

Singing in the Struggles

One of the ways Cyndi worships her heavenly Father is through writing—whether it be poems, songs, or insights He gives her as she's dealing with life.

"Everything that has ever happened, small or big, I've been able to say 'God is going to be able to use this. I'm going to be able to comfort someone who needs comforting. I'm going to be able to relate to someone else in this pain.' All these things have brought out in me an ability to express myself."

And she does that through her poetry—an offering of praise to her Creator and Lord, in spite of all that life has brought. When she and her husband moved to a new city recently, Cyndi had been telling herself over and over that the joy of the Lord was her strength. She repeated this truth from Nehemiah 8:10 as she was daily adjusting to new surroundings and the loss of easy access to her friends, family, and everything familiar.

"As I continued to say this verse over and over to myself, I wanted to know more about what it really meant. I had to put some descriptions to it and wanted to create a picture in my mind that I could see and hold onto tightly. I asked God to show me what it meant that He was my strength, and He put these words on my heart:

The Joy—God's Joy—What does this look like?
How does God express His Joy?
He Sings over me
He Delights in me
He Laughs and Smiles over me
He Bends down to listen and to whisper His love in my ear.
He Shares His heart with me and He Reminds me that I am His!
He Extends His hand to me—inviting me to sup with Him.
He Covers me and Carries me
He Waits patiently for me to call him LORD.
He Showers me with Grace and pours Mercy on my walking path.
He Rejoices over my obedience and rest in Him.
This Joy is vast, it is deep and it is unending!
It is perpetual, everlasting, and unshakeable.
It is in motion, and it is always active!
This Joy is His—yet it is mine,
for He is mine and I am His—
and THIS is my strength![1]

Cyndi has shared that poem—and others she's written—with friends who have needed focus, with caretakers of the elderly, with some who were dying, and with many who just needed to be encouraged to rely on God's strength, especially when their own has run dry.

Cyndi's ability to praise God in her pain is not unique. A woman who is able to overcome life's hurts is a woman who is able to see God's good in her grievances. She takes what God has allowed in her life and uses it for His glory. For Cyndi, sharing her poems and insights with others, or just having them written down as an act of obedience and praise, is a reminder to her to see every obstacle in her life as an opportunity to grow spiritually. As she sought to be obedient, praise resulted. And through the praise she—and others—have found joy.

More Examples of Joy in the Midst of Hurt

Listen to the words of other women who have been hurt yet found reason to rejoice.

Discovering Her Uniqueness

When Susan was a child, she was told by her father that she would never measure up.

"I grew up in a Christian home with a very strict father and a mother who was an adult child of an alcoholic. She was and is a saint and endured what I observed to be a marriage that was strained. My dad loved my mom but didn't treat her with much respect. And yet he told me in my teen years that I would never be the woman my mom was. Wow, that was deeply hurtful. I don't know what I did to deserve that. I was an A-student, a (mostly) compliant child, the first of five children (all the others were boys) who helped quite a bit around the house and participated in all church activities with a willing heart. So, you can imagine how sad that made me. My dad didn't think I'd become much of a woman.

"It took a while for me to get over the urge to prove him wrong. It took quite a long time before I realized that I could not become 'the woman my mother was' because I was a unique creation of God's. I would become the woman God made me to be, the woman whom I was meant to be, a unique beloved daughter of the King of kings. This realization was, of course, very freeing.

"I adore my mom. She is an incredible woman of God, but we are so different! She never had the opportunity to go to college. I graduated and entered the workforce, whereas she has always been a stay-at-home wife and mom. I continue to work outside my home and consider the corporate environment my mission field. She is the consummate home-maker: She cooks, she cleans, she sews, she entertains. I am marginal at those tasks, but have other gifts. That very hurtful comment from my dad was devastating, but it spurred me on to become the person *God* wanted me to be without becoming the victim of a difficult relationship."

Today Susan is a women's ministry leader who finds joy in serving God and others. She has a beautiful voice, a beautiful spirit, and is a woman through whom the joy of the Lord shines.

Experiencing God's Peace and Provision

Throughout her life, Denise believed she was a disappointment to God and herself because of the choices she had made. "I made choices in my life based upon the fear of being an inconvenience to others," she said.

At 22 years old, she had an abortion. The father was her boyfriend, whom she married 14 months later. Although she immediately regretted her decision to end her pregnancy, for more than 20 years she never told anyone (except the baby's father) what had happened. So she couldn't turn to anyone for help in dealing with her pain. She started a family at age 26 and, after giving birth to a healthy son and daughter, she was surprised to find herself pregnant again at 30. Her baby girl was born premature and medically fragile. The little girl had a successful bone marrow transplant at age 3, but she continued to have health struggles until she died at age 9 1/2. Then Denise's 13-year-old son began to struggle with deep depression and suicidal thoughts.

Then just as life finally started to smooth out, Denise's husband of 22 years left her. He had kept an affair secret from her for several months, and he left her at the time she was just beginning to deal with the wounds caused by her abortion 23 years earlier.

Today at 50, Denise says, "God has given me great peace in the midst of the grief of losing my daughter. And God has brought me through the fear and hurt of divorce, He provided me with a church family that loves me, a career that provides for my physical needs, and a deep, steadfast knowledge that I am not an inconvenience to Him."

Celebrating Newness of Life

At 35 years old, Misty no longer struggles with what she once believed were visible wounds of a past lifestyle. For Misty, dancing in the adult entertainment industry began as a way to survive. Her boyfriend had just broken up with her and moved out, and she had three days to come up with the rent, plus a little girl to take care of. She was scared, desperate, hurt, and felt alone in facing the world.

"I was no stranger to heartbreak and bad relationships," Misty said. "By this time I had already been lied to, cheated on, and shown over and over again that I wasn't good enough or worth staying for. Dancing seemed like a great way to make the money I needed to support us, and it would also allow me to stay home during the day and raise my daughter. I wanted to prove that I didn't need anyone to take care of me, especially the guy who had just left me!" By dancing, Misty was able to pay her rent in a couple nights and she began telling myself she was strong and independent for doing so.

"In the beginning, I spent my money however I wanted because I knew I could go back and replace it that night. I was able to provide in ways I never had before, and thought I had truly found freedom in life. However, this freedom came with a *huge* price."

Misty's hope of being independent and being able to pay the bills led instead to a deep bondage, depression, and drug addiction.

"I found out very quickly how to play the game and I created a whole new identity for myself. I thought I could pull off living two totally different lifestyles—one as a responsible, loving, stay-at-home mom [to her two children by then] and the other as a crazy, fun, carefree girl. I lost me in the mix and eventually addiction took over. Not just drug addiction to painkillers to numb me and get me through the night, but also addiction to the praise, compliments, money, lifestyle, gifts, trips, and parties. Over time, I lost touch with reality. I started using drugs I had sworn I would never touch. I started lying to everyone around me and denying that I had a problem with anything. I found myself living in a vicious cycle that lasted for ten years. It was a horrible repetitious cycle and I did not know how to make it stop."

Through a series of devastating events, Misty finally cried out to God. Then she confided in a friend that she needed help, and two days later moved into a safe home. A Christian family that had opened their home to her offered to take her to church. There, she heard the pastor speak from the Bible, and she saw the verses on a screen in the front of the church. That is when God's Word began to penetrate her heart.

"As I read the verses and listened to what he was saying, it felt as if every single word was written just for me. It spoke to my broken, lifeless soul. I knew I wanted and needed more. I could not get enough of the words, the promises, and the truths that were filling up every crack of my broken heart. With every word I read, life and hope started entering my soul again.

"I started getting to know who Jesus is more than just reading about Him. The family I lived with was an amazing reflection of Him and I took notice and was drawn to it. I wanted that joy, peace, and balance for my own life and the lives of my children. I had so much regret and it was painful to think of all the destruction I had caused to so many lives. I cried and told God I wanted to make things right. I asked Him to forgive me. I started looking at myself and the choices I had made that led up to my horrific fall. I took ownership and responsibility for my part in everything. I faced things about myself that I hadn't wanted to face for years. Although it was not pretty, I finally faced the truth and stopped running.

"The lies I had believed about myself started to be replaced with truth. I had been searching for love and acceptance my entire life but it always eluded me. I tried everything there was in the world to fill that emptiness and could never figure out why nothing ever worked or lasted. I put impossible expectations on people and I searched constantly for someone to 'rescue' me.

"I am happy to say that I have been *rescued*! Rescued from my misery and set free from all the lies. I finally found that the answer isn't pain pills, money, attention, or what anyone else is selling—it's Jesus Christ! He has made me whole. The emptiness that once controlled me and led me down a path of destruction has now been filled by God's *real* love!

"Now that I have placed my faith in God and given all my life to Him, He is transforming everything! My relationships are being restored, and I am now able to be a good mother for my two children. He is changing my heart and the way I see this world. I no longer want to chase after things that don't satisfy. My desires are now for things that are healthier and more positive. I now live a life that is full of meaning and purpose. My pain has now developed into a passion to help others."

Today, Misty is putting that purpose and passion to work by ministering to other women who want to escape the bondage of the sex industry. (You'll hear more about how her life has become a blessing to others in the next chapter.)

She, too, was able to find her song in all the suffering: "I'm so thankful I finally found God after 34 years of wrecking myself. Today

I am watching and trusting Him as He makes my life beautiful and I'm at the most peace I have ever been."

Susan, Denise, and Misty are three different women, with different sets of wounds, from three different places in life. Yet they are all able to see that in their pain, God was bringing about something worthy of praise.

Becoming a Woman of Praise

How can *you* be a woman who worships, and not just a woman who is wounded? How can you, in a practical way, praise God through the pain and see His joy flood into your life?

Consider His Character

Cyndi's ability to cope with life's losses and hurts is a direct result of her deep knowledge of the character of God.

"Most of us don't really know God, which is why we worry and don't trust giving Him the reins of our life," Cyndi said. "Are you staying where you are in life because you've bought a lie, or because you don't know your Savior very well?

"We get into Bible studies and we study, study, study but we don't have this deep, abiding knowledge and assurance of who God is." She said she studied the names of God to understand His character and His love. Now when reading Scripture, "the power of who God is and the strength of His great name jump off the pages and become alive and tangible! I learned if I start here and learn who it is I believe in, then I can move forward."[2]

Consider It Joy

We are instructed in James 1:2-4 to "consider it all joy, my brethren, when you encounter various trials, knowing that the testing of your faith produces endurance. And let endurance have its perfect result, that you may be perfect and complete, lacking in nothing."[3] When we have our eye on the prize—becoming "perfect and complete, lacking in nothing"—we can consider our difficult times joyful. That doesn't mean you put on a phony smile and grit your teeth through it. It means you endure through the trial with a deep inner peace and assurance that God is refining you and making you into the woman He desires you to be.

A few years ago when Cyndi was in the hospital with meningitis, she recalls "lying there in God's arms with pain so great and out of control—yet knowing I wasn't abandoned. He used me in my pain. He loved me as I cried. He taught me as I waited. He never left my side. My nights were often long and the days seemed even longer. Though few could understand, it didn't seem to bother me. It was my time to listen and learn of Him—to be captured and molded from within."

The awareness that God has "captured" us and is "molding" us from within is what brings us joy.

I endured a dark time of testing recently. I felt I was being spiritually attacked at every corner. I wondered, for a brief time, if God had abandoned me. (I didn't really, but you know that voice that whispers, "Where is your God during a time like this?" Well, I was hearing that voice.)

Then in a Sunday morning sermon my husband preached on Peter's instructions to stand firm in our faith (from 1 Peter 5:8-10) and reminded us that Jesus personally told Peter earlier in his life, "Satan has demanded permission to sift you like wheat; but I have prayed for you, that your strength may not fail" (Luke 22:31-32 NASB). I was reminded that Satan had to get permission from Jesus to sift Peter, and Jesus had granted that permission knowing He was going to give Peter the strength he needed to withstand that testing. What an encouragement for me to realize that anytime you and I experience spiritual attack it is because our Lord has allowed it, and is intending to give us the strength we need to endure it. (There's a parallel account in the Old Testament book of Job, where we read that Satan asked permission to sift and test Job. Our gracious and loving God allowed it because He knew His faithful servant Job would pass the test.) My perspective changed completely that morning. I realized that if God is allowing this "sifting" in my life, He must know His daughter can handle it (with His help, of course).

Consider It Loss

We can praise God while experiencing loss in our life if we aren't holding too tightly onto our possessions or what we feel we have a right to keep.

Cyndi knows that mentality because of the losses she has endured, especially the material losses as of late. During her time in Texas she has endured a couple of hurricanes, which has taught her to walk away from the stuff and focus on what really matters.

"When Hurricane Rita hit Texas (right after Hurricane Katrina hit Louisiana), we packed our cats and whatever we could fit in our car and just drove away. It was the eeriest feeling to think I might not see anybody and anything again," she said.

"It was a lonely feeling, too, as I sat in someone else's house and watched the television coverage of my town being demolished. I wondered, *Did my house make it? Is there anything left of what I have?*"

When Hurricane Ike struck a few years later, Cyndi and her husband stayed in town and ministered to people in the community. By then they realized that their stuff would be damaged or lost, and that caring for people was more important. Those two hurricane experiences taught Cyndi what really matters in life.

"I now have the hurricane mentality," she said. "I have learned to just walk away and let things go. I now tell people, 'Just get a hurricane mentality—be willing to part with it.'"

In Philippians 3:8, the apostle Paul said that everything he worked for in life—all his titles, honors, achievements, and prestige—meant nothing in comparison to knowing Christ. In fact, he said, "I consider everything a loss because of the surpassing worth of knowing Christ Jesus my Lord, for whose sake I have lost all things. I consider them garbage, that I may gain Christ" (NIV).

If all that you have—your health, your home, your possessions, your job, your titles, and your achievements—is considered loss in comparison to what you have in your relationship with Christ, you will be able to praise God during those losses, remembering that "the God of all grace, who called you to His eternal glory in Christ, will Himself perfect, confirm, strengthen and establish you" (1 Peter 5:10 NASB).

Cultivate a Heart of Trust

When we are trusting God to provide for us, there is no room for pity or worry, only praise. Jesus instructed us to "not worry about your life, what you will eat or what you will drink; nor about your body, what you will put on...Look at the birds of the air, for they neither sow nor reap nor gather into barns; yet your heavenly Father feeds them. Are you not of more value that they?" (Matthew 6:25-26). We are also instructed in Philippians 4:6-7 to "Be anxious for nothing, but in everything by prayer and supplication, with thanksgiving, let your requests be made known to God, and the peace of God, which surpasses all understanding, will guard your hearts and minds through Christ Jesus."

Cyndi has claimed these verses as her own and relied on them often. She says, "I love it when, in the Psalms, David declares that God has brought him up from the slimy pit and placed his feet on a solid rock [Psalm 40:2], and made his lot secure [Psalm 16:5], or brought him out into a spacious place [Psalm 18:19]. I have been in that pit many times and have been delivered victoriously!"

Cyndi said one Scripture verse that has been like preventative medicine for her is Psalm 37:4: "Delight yourself in the LORD; and He will give you the desires of your heart."[4]

"A heart of gratitude, despite the moment, is like a protective shield around that pit," she said. "That tells me I must start with a habit, a good habit, which will produce a good attitude, and then a heart change toward all that is happening around me.

"Many, many times I would run to a quiet place—whether it was a closet, a bathroom, or my car—and pour out my tears with only these words: 'I choose to trust You, God.' It was all I could say and all that needed to be said. He heard the rest in my heart and He knew that I came empty to Him, with only what He needed to hear from me, so that I could see Him move mountains and lay the valleys low. Those words were a habit before they were an attitude or a deeply rooted belief, but I was planting a seed in my heart that I desperately wanted to grow! I knew the alternative would send me deeper into despair and back into that pit and I also knew that Satan wanted me to fold to him, so those words were my battle cry. And my victorious Savior came every time I called."

Let the Praises Flow

If you have ever wondered about God's will for your life, it is for you to praise Him in your pain. In 1 Thessalonians 5:18 we are told, "In everything give thanks; for this is the will of God in Christ Jesus for you."

Did you catch that? *In everything* give thanks. In sickness. In heartache. In physical pain. In times of lack or loss. In *all things*, sing. And when you praise God in your pain, sing to Him in your struggles, and lift Him up when you're loaded down, you are not only doing what delights Him, you are *becoming* His delight.

In everything give thanks, my friend. And joy will flow into your life and out to others.

STEP #9 *Toward Healing and Wholeness*

Refresh your soul by praising God in your pain.

Becoming grateful to God in everything is the primary way to live out God's will for you.

LET THE HEALING CONTINUE

Let's apply the steps from this chapter on becoming a woman of praise:

1. *Consider His character*—Read Psalm 18:30-36 and write a praise-filled response to God:

2. *Consider it joy*—Read James 1:2-4 and list below all the situations in your life that God is calling you to "consider it joy" right now because of how He is shaping your character through it.

3. *Consider it loss*—Paul said in Philippians 3:7-8 that all he had gained in this life was like garbage compared to the value of knowing Christ. How can you adopt a "hurricane mentality" when it comes to your possessions, your titles, and even your achievements, as a way of saying "You, Lord, are worth far more than any of this"?

4. *Cultivate a heart of trust*—Read Philippians 4:6-7. In what area of your life do you need to practice this instruction?

A Prayer of Praise for His Healing

Where do I start, O God, when it comes to recounting Your goodness? Yes, my heart hurts from the pain I've endured. Yet Your comforting touch has always been there. Yes, my eyes still tear up when I think of past regrets or people I loved who are no longer in my life, but You, O Lord, have never left my side. Yes, there has been sorrow that has seemed like one long night. But You have promised that joy will come, just as surely as the morning (Psalm 30:5).

Lord, I praise You for all You have allowed into my life to make me more like You. And because You have said, "To obey is better than sacrifice" (1 Samuel 15:22), I will offer You the sacrifice of praise from an obedient heart.

Give me the strength and the song so I can, in all things, sing—in order to please Your heart and share with others about the wondrous God that You are. And please pour Your joy over my soul as I praise You from the center of my pain.

I Can Be a Blessing

Reinvesting in the Lives of Others

Tonia Tewell lay in a hospital bed, aware that she was dying.

She was 36 years old, but was feeling the weight of a life wasted. She remembers telling God, "Please don't take me now. I've done *nothing* for You. If You give me a week, if You give me a month, if You give me a year, I will serve You boldly."

The doctors then came in and delivered the devastating news: She had terminal cancer—lymphoma in her neck, chest, groin, and intestinal tract. Stage Four cancer. It was pretty much over.

She immediately started chemotherapy. But instead of a determination to live, she was determined to serve others before she died.

"My friends were crying, my husband had a breakdown, but I had complete peace," Tonia recalled. "I knew I couldn't go this way because I hadn't done anything for the Lord. I knew it wasn't a prerequisite for His love or His salvation, but I had done *nothing* for Him because I was afraid of failing."

Tonia lived with fear from the time she was a child. Her fear of failure resulted from an underlying fear of upsetting her two alcoholic parents. She feared that she and her brother and sister would be killed in the middle of the night by an abusive mother who, as a raging alcoholic, carried a gun and was often drunk at night. She feared that during one of the many parties her parents held, she or her brother or sister would be harmed by the predators who attended those parties.

By the time Tonia was in seventh grade, fear for the future set in as she and her younger sister and brother had been abandoned by both their parents.

"All three of us got called into the principal's office. We had never met him before. He said, 'You three are being given up to the state; however, I won't let that happen to you. I will take you *all* in if I have to, but I will find homes for you.'"

The principal and his wife took Tonia into their home and she knew, at that age, that for her to have a normal life she had to stay there.

"They were a wonderful family," she said. "They were so normal and stable it was uncomfortable. I kept waiting for the other shoe to drop, I kept waiting for them to reject me and walk away. I just wanted to get it over with. But they never left. They were my saving grace. They still are today."

Tonia enrolled in college and shortly thereafter began looking for whatever would self-gratify—drinking, men, drugs, becoming a University of Nebraska cheerleader.

"I woke up one morning after a near-overdose and felt like I was going to die. I realized I needed to change my way of life," she said. She attempted to do that on her own by concentrating on her grades and giving up partying and men. She met her husband about a year later. Although he was a great man, their marriage was terrible, she said. She found a saving relationship with Christ at 30 years old. But her marriage got worse after she became a believer. "My husband had a mental breakdown and tried to prove I was in a cult," Tonia said. But three years later, he found a saving relationship through Christ as well.

Facing Her Fears

Shortly after her husband found Christ, God began preparing Tonia and her husband for what lay ahead, beginning with Tonia's diagnosis of Stage Four cancer. It was then that she told God she would put aside her fears of failure in order to serve Him with what little time she had left.

"I started serving people, in that condition, and they were just floored," Tonia said. "As I was lying in line for chemo, my husband and I would be comforting people, praying for them, talking about our faith. I had Christian friends and my family with me. Most people were there alone while fighting for their lives."

Tonia was told that she would know her life expectancy based on when her cancer returned, which the doctors expected would be about three to five years. It returned with a vengeance the following year.

"I knew I'd be on chemo and drugs for the rest of my life," Tonia said. "I knew the drugs would kill me before the cancer did. So I walked away from the medical community to just enjoy my remaining days." Tonia went on a strict diet of raw fruits and vegetables and seeds, and she continued to serve God as best she could in her fragile condition. Less than two months later she ended up in the emergency room.

"I thought, *I'm an idiot* [for having walked away from medical help]. *The cancer has spread everywhere. I'm gonna die soon.*"

By the time Tonia's medical scan was completed, her pain was gone, and she was told that her cancer was gone as well.

That was four years ago. According to Tonia's doctors, she should have expired two years ago.

Realizing she had a new lease on life, Tonia went through a process of trying to determine what God wanted her to do with the time He had given her.

"I was asked to be a part of women's ministry. I thought, *This is it.* Then someone asked me to speak. I spoke a couple times, and thought, *Maybe this is it.* Someone then came to our church and made us aware of the polygamy taking place in our community [Tonia lives in a suburb of Salt Lake City, Utah]. This person asked if someone had a safe house for women and children and men transitioning out of polygamy."

Tonia's family had already purchased a much bigger house to accommodate her family coming in to help her, an extra room for a live-in nurse during her last days of cancer, and quarters for a live-in nanny to care for her children after she passed. Now that her cancer was gone, she and her family were living in a house with an extra 2500 square feet on the lower level that they weren't even using. Tonia told the woman looking for a safe house, "We have room!"

Tonia received a call shortly afterward in which she was informed that a mother, a daughter, and the daughter's four children needed a place to stay. The Tewell family welcomed them into their home for the summer.

"What an incredible summer our family had," Tonia said. "What an eye-opener. We had meetings every night with this family that was suffering from severe anxiety. We were helping domestic refugees who were terrified. At the end of the summer they sat us down and said, 'We've never felt unconditional love like this.'

"This family asked us if we would start an organization to help them and several families they knew who needed help escaping from a polyg-amist lifestyle."

Tonia's doubts and insecurities then came to the surface again.

"I was a stay-at-home mom for ten years. I had no skills to start an organization and didn't feel qualified in the least. But we set out on a fact-finding mission and it was clear there were no resources for these people, so with God's help, we started Holding Out HELP (Helping Encouraging and Loving Polygamists).

Since Holding Out HELP (HOH) began in 2008, it has served more than 180 people and has more than 30 safe homes all over the nation, although most teens and families fleeing polygamy prefer to stay in Utah, specifically Salt Lake City or St. George. The organiza-tion is now in the beginning stages of a fundraising campaign to pur-chase a boarding home and apartments to serve the rapidly increasing numbers of youth and families who are leaving the Fundamental Lat-ter Day Saints movement and are depending on HOH to meet their immediate needs.[1]

By helping others find freedom from their oppressed lifestyle, Tonia has found freedom as well from the bondage of fear that held her cap-tive for years.

"Ultimately, only Jesus can free us," Tonia said. "And I know that. When I realized what He had done for me on the cross—*me*, in spite of my *entire life*—I had to hand my life over to Him.

"Today, when things are too difficult for me to handle, I lay them at the feet of Jesus because I know He can handle them. It's a process of total surrender. I don't suffer so much with my childhood; I suffer more from feelings of inadequacy.

"When I started Holding Out HELP I was completely overwhelmed and I started having anxiety attacks again. I hadn't had those in years. I realized I was trying to control things and that I needed to surrender this to God and I needed to be in prayer and in the Word more. Every time this organization has made a prayer request, I have seen an answer of some kind or another within twenty-four to forty-eight hours."

Tonia—the once-fearful, abused, and eventually abandoned child—now offers a safe place for those who are seeking freedom from fearful and abusive situations. She has found freedom, healing, and wholeness by investing in the lives of others.

The Common Thread

As we near the end of this journey, I hope you have noticed the common thread in each woman's story I've told throughout this book. As wounded as each one once was, she found her purpose through her pain. She let her loss motivate her to love others. And she once was *hurting* and now she's *helping* someone else.

Today, they are no longer wounded women. They are *warrior* women—out on the front lines of the spiritual battle for women's hearts so other women can find healing and wholeness too. Ephesians 6:12 tells us, "We do not wrestle against flesh and blood, but against principalities, against powers, against the rulers of the darkness of this age, against spiritual hosts of wickedness in the heavenly places."

The number of women who suffer from childhood pain, past hurts, and present heartaches and the lingering residue of rejection and abuse indicates to us that the spiritual battle that exists for their hearts and lives is more intense than we may realize. Women aren't just getting over it. They are often stuck in the battle, remaining in a place where they are continually defeated, perpetually wounded, hopelessly broken. But as God heals *us* and makes us whole, He also equips us to re-enter and fight that battle, rather than surrender to it, in order to help pull *others* from the carnage.

In chapter 1, you read about the battlefront of Ivonne's home life. She was wounded and desperate to get out of her house and find a different life. And one caring woman took her in. Today, Ivonne is that one caring woman offering counsel and comfort for countless other teenagers who are experiencing some of the same struggles she did.

In the second chapter you met Sharon, who was deeply scarred from the battleground of physical and sexual abuse by her father. Then she endured a painful marriage. Then she had not one, but two bouts of cancer. All her life she felt broken and unwanted. Yet she has emerged from the scars and today celebrates the healing and wholeness of women, assuring them of their beauty, significance, and worth in the eyes of a loving God.

Christina, whose deliverance from the pit was told in the third chapter and whose wisdom is sprinkled throughout this book, found Christ in a tiny little Vacation Bible School program on the back side of the Southern California desert. And today she directs a Vacation Bible School program ministering to hundreds of children, including the forgotten, seemingly unwanted children who live like she once did. And today when she speaks, she shares an inspiring message of hope that God can redeem *anyone* from the pit and provide victory on *any* battlefield.

Natasha (in chapter 5) and Carol and Jan (in chapter 7) also received battle scars in their fight to survive the emotional pain of growing up without a loving father. Today they are beacons of hope in the lives of others who are benefitting from the healing they have experienced as well as their personal stories of redemption.

Jill Kelly (chapter 6) endured the pain of watching her son battle Krabbe disease and now heads up Hunter's Hope—an organization that provides encouragement and help to other families of children suffering the effects of Krabbe disease and related leukodystrophies.

Cyndi, whose story of enduring much loss was told in the previous chapter, encourages others through her writings that point to God as the Maker, Sustainer, and Source of Strength for all of us no matter what we've been through.

And Misty, who struggled for ten years to get out of the adult entertainment industry, now helps rescue other women out of the bondage she once experienced. She has founded You Are a Jewel ministry, a faith-based organization and support group for women who are currently or have been in the adult entertainment industry or are victims of sexual exploitation or human sexual trafficking.

"We visit the strip clubs here in Salt Lake City and bring gifts to the girls, along with the message that they are loved and valued. Most are there because of life's hurts, and we encourage them toward learning the truth about themselves."[2]

These women were able to overcome their own hurts and then step into the battle that other women around them were facing and help them find refuge. They were able to do all that when they realized to whom they belong, and to whom they owe their lives.

Strength for the Battle

The strength we need to overcome life's hurts and stand firm in the battle that rages around us is found through intimacy with Jesus Christ.

Strength through intimacy? Yes. It's another one of those paradoxes in Scripture. Jesus instructed us to abide (or dwell continually) with Him because "without Me you can do nothing" (John 15:5). We are also told in Ephesians 6:10-17 to put on the full armor of God so that we can take our stand against the devil's schemes. Every memory that comes back to haunt you, every feeling of resentment that surfaces in your soul, every careless comment that triggers an insecurity that starts to take you back down a dark path could be schemes of the devil designed to ensnare you to your wounds once more. So you need to "extinguish all the flaming arrows of the evil one"[3] so you can continue to stand firm and fight valiantly in this battle that seeks to destroy our hearts and minds.

So how do you remain in Christ and put on the full armor of God so you can extinguish the fiery arrows and have victory in this battle? Scripture mentions two ways we can defend against the enemy's attacks:

1. Capture Every Thought

Our minds can be an intense battlefield, and some of our biggest wars are fought there. So it is essential that we learn how to corral and capture every thought that runs wild in our heads—every thought that reminds us of something we want to forget, or brings us back to a place where we don't want to go. In 2 Corinthians 10:4-5, the apostle Paul wrote,

> The weapons we fight with are not the weapons of the world. On the contrary, they have divine power to demolish strongholds. We demolish arguments and every pretension that sets itself up against the knowledge of God, and we take captive every thought to make it obedient to Christ (NIV).

You can do this in a practical way by praying, as soon as a thought comes into your mind, that the thought would be released if it's not pleasing to God. Filter it through the mind of Christ in you. Philippians 4:8 explains how to do that:

> Whatever is true, whatever is noble, whatever is right, whatever is pure, whatever is lovely, whatever is admirable—if anything is excellent or praiseworthy—think about such things (NIV).

If the thought taunting you or the memory making its way into your mind doesn't meet the above criteria, it has no place in your mind. It is part of the "old things [that] have passed away" (2 Corinthians 5:17).

The second way to defend yourself is to watch how you dress.

2. Clothe Yourself in Christ

Scripture tells us in Ephesians 6:10 to "be strong in the Lord and in the power of His might." How is this done? We find the answer in the next few verses:

> Put on the full armor of God, so that when the day of evil comes, you may be able to stand your ground, and after you have done everything, to stand. Stand firm then, with the belt of truth buckled around your waist, with the breastplate of righteousness in place, and with your feet fitted with the readiness that comes from the gospel

of peace. In addition to all this, take up the shield of faith, with which you can extinguish all the flaming arrows of the evil one. Take the helmet of salvation and the sword of the spirit, which is the word of God.

And pray in the Spirit on all occasions with all kinds of prayers and requests. With this in mind, be alert and always keep on praying for all the Lord's people (Ephesians 6:13-18 NIV).

In that passage we have a detailed description of how to suit up to defeat the "roaring lion looking for someone to devour" (1 Peter 5:8 NIV). If you pay close attention to what the passage says, you will realize that putting on the armor of God is synonymous with clothing yourself in the character of Jesus Christ, or simply *abiding* in Him. Each piece of the armor makes reference to an aspect of Christ's character. So when you are told to stand firm with the *belt of truth* buckled around your waist, you can know confidently that at the core of your being should be Jesus—who is the *truth*, as described in John 14:6. To put on the *breastplate of righteousness* means to cover your heart or clothe yourself in Christ, who is called "The LORD our Righteousness" in Jeremiah 23:6. To put on your *helmet of salvation* is to guard your head or mind with Christ because "salvation is found in no one else" (Acts 4:12 NIV). In other words, to put Christ at your core, over your heart, and over your mind is to remain or abide or dwell intimately with Him.

The Example of Jesus

We've talked in previous chapters about how we can become more like Christ through our sufferings that have shaped and molded our character. But have you ever thought of how you are like Christ simply because you've been hurt by this world?

Sharon thinks about that often. Sharon, whose story is told in chapter 2, longed for a loving God throughout her painful childhood and finally found Him as an adult. Yet she recognizes, in knowing what Christ went through for her, that she is more like Him because of the wounds she has suffered. In fact, she sees her life as "an incredible opportunity to walk in Christ's footsteps."

"For me, there's a healing in being wounded," she said. "When we go through the wounds and we get to the other side, that's the life that Christ walked. He was perfect. He came here to walk through the pain and suffering that all of us go through in life and then He died, only to live again. I was born into an imperfect world too, and was wounded as a result."

And because Christ died and rose again to bring healing and hope—spiritually, physically and emotionally—Sharon can live again too. And so can you.

"It's not even about getting through the wounds and getting to the other side," Sharon said. "It's about embracing the wounds so you can minister to others. There's hardly a hurt that someone else has experienced that I can't relate to. That is now a gift."

Can you see *your* hurts in life as a gift because of how they shaped you and made you into a woman who is able to relate to and minister to others? The Bible tells us that God comforts us so we in turn may comfort others:

> Praise be to the God and Father of our Lord Jesus Christ, the Father of compassion and the God of all comfort, who comforts us in all our troubles, so that we can comfort those in any trouble with the comfort we ourselves receive from God (2 Corinthians 1:3-4 NIV).

Ivonne, Sharon, Christina, and all the women whose stories are included in this book will tell you that their sufferings have shaped their character and not only helped them relate to other women who are experiencing pain, but equipped them to minister to those women as well.

Their sufferings have also helped them relate to Jesus as a "Man of sorrows" (Isaiah 53:3) who is the hope and light of nations (Isaiah 51:4). They see in Him a pattern they want to live out as well. Jesus endured rejection, betrayal, personal insults, false accusations, physical torture, and the excruciating emotional pain of momentary separation from His Father (that last one is, by the way, something *you* will never have to experience if you are in a saving relationship with Jesus Christ). Jesus endured all of that to bring us healing and wholeness—physically, emotionally, and spiritually. He suffered to bring us life. And likewise, through *our* suffering, we can offer hope and a new way of life to others.

Sharon said once we've been healed, once we've made it to the other side, "the responsibility is huge."

"Now that I've been healed and restored, if I'm not sharing that, then I'm not doing His work."

It's Your Turn

As we come to the end of our journey together, I want to leave you with a step-by-step process for turning your hurt into hope for others. Perhaps you're still wondering where and how to minister to someone else. Maybe your pain is still so fresh you can't imagine being in a place where you can help others. But God is already working *in* you the redemptive work He wants to accomplish in others *through* you.

1. Look Backward—At Where He's Brought You

Look back so you can remember how far God has brought you and where you'd be were it not for His healing hand and tender touch. But don't dwell there. As Oswald Chambers said: "Beware of paying attention or going back to what you once were, when God wants you to be something that you have never been."[4]

Looking back should serve as a motivation for making sure you never return to that place. It should propel you forward to take greater strides. If it helps, write out, in a journal, what God delivered you from or, if it's too early to tell, write about what you are experiencing now in the Lord's deliverance.

2. Look Inward—At What He's Done in You

What has God developed in you during your hurts that can now be poured out to others? Has He cultivated in you character traits that could encourage or build up others? Has He given you a greater compassion for children who are being treated as you once were? Has He put women on your heart who have been betrayed by their husbands? Has He burdened you with the single mother and all that she has to bear? By asking yourself "What do I feel strongly about?" and "Whom can I reach out to?" you can get at the core work that God has woven into you through your wounds.

3. Look Outward—At Those Who Need Help

Jesus said "to whom much is given, from him much will be required" (Luke 12:48). Have you received much healing? Offer it to others as well. Have you received much grace and forgiveness? Extend it to others too. Have you found Him to be your hope in your darkness? Help others find His light as well.

We can help others simply by sharing our story. Some of us walk around talking way too much about everything that went wrong in our lives. That's not what I'm suggesting here. I'm talking about telling others what God has done in your life. There's a difference. Rather than elaborating on the darkness, emphasize His deliverance. Rather than stressing the hurts, spotlight the Healer. Rather than making it about yourself, make it about Him. As you begin to talk about Jesus and what He did in you and what He's willing to do in someone else, others will want to hear about it—not just those who have been through similar circumstances, but anyone who needs to hear of hope. When you begin telling your story, God will draw others toward you who need your hope and encouragement.

4. Look Upward—for His Strength and Equipping

Even after God has delivered you from painful situations, you must constantly depend on His strength, His timing, and His enablement so you can minister to the hearts of other women. It's never about you. It's all too easy to slip and think, *Wow, I'm doing some great things for people.* But your focus must be like John the Baptist's as he saw Jesus' popularity growing at the expense of his own ministry. John humbly said, "He must increase, but I must decrease" (John 3:30). There is no hope or healing in any of us. It is only Christ *through us* that makes a difference in the lives of others.

Philippians 4:13 says, "I can do all things through Christ who strengthens me." Make that your motto, and that will help you keep your eyes on the One who makes all things possible.

5. Look Forward—to the Doors God Will Open

As happened with Tonia, you might not find your ministry to others by trying this and that. It's possible God will take you by surprise with a ministry opportunity that falls into your lap. Whatever the case, you want to be open to the opportunities that present themselves and be willing to walk through whatever doors God swings open for you.

Because Deanna (in chapter 8) was able to forgive her husband, Brian, for his unfaithfulness to her, the two of them now help other struggling couples through their small group ministry at church. They have told their story to offer hope to others that forgiveness is, in fact, possible. But Deanna never would have voluntarily signed up to do something like that. She ended up in that role because she was responsive to God's work in her life and obedient to His nudge when an opportunity was presented.

Anne, whose story is similar to Deanna's, had a chance to forgive, face-to-face, her former best friend, who committed adultery with her husband. Through events she believes were God-ordained, the two women now have a restored and an even richer friendship than they had before. How is that possible?

"The turn of events was a miracle in itself and I am forever grateful for how things have worked out," Anne said. "God turns devastating decisions into endless possibilities; at least that is what I have learned over and over as I go along in life. When I tell people just a fraction of all the things God has done over the last nine years, I feel like it gives hope to seemingly hopeless situations."

There are countless people out there looking for hope. Can your story shine some light of hope into their darkness? Then tell it.

The Voices of Victory

Cyndi shared with me the words that came to her as she reflected on the life we can offer to others through the losses we experience:

> Let it go—let it die
> The hurts, the pain, the problems—
> The injustice, the guilt, the sentencing.

Let it go—let it die so Life can come forth from within.
New Life in abundance—so rich and free.
New Life that reaches beyond you and me.[5]

Do you see now how our lives can be even more like our Lord's when we take what we've been given—and what we've lost—and offer it back to God as a sacrifice of service and praise? If our hurts help others, then we have, in a sense, been Jesus to someone else. And we have seen a glimpse of what we were designed to be and how we were designed to live.

Let the Rivers Flow

Do you realize there is a source of living water in you that Christ has cultivated and wants to nourish others with? Jesus said in John 7:38, "He who believes in Me, as the Scripture has said, out of his heart will flow rivers of living water."

As one writer put it:

> A river reaches places which its source never knows. And Jesus said that, if we have received His fullness, "rivers of living water" will flow out of us, reaching in blessing even "to the ends of the earth" (Acts 1:8) regardless of how small the visible effects of our lives may appear to be. We have nothing to do with the outflow—"This is the work of God, that you believe..." (John 6:29). God rarely allows a person to see how great a blessing he is to others.[6]
>
> Think of the healing and far-reaching rivers developing and nourishing themselves in our souls! God has been opening up wonderful truths to our minds, and every point He has opened up is another indication of the wider power of the river that He will flow through us. If you believe in Jesus, you will find that God has developed and nourished in you mighty, rushing rivers of blessing for others.[7]

These rushing rivers of blessing are one of the treasures we received while walking through the darkness. God tells us:

> I will give you the treasures of darkness
> And hidden wealth of secret places,
> So that you may know that it is I,
> The LORD, the God of Israel, who calls you by your name
> (Isaiah 45:3 NASB).

You have been given a wealth of riches in the deep hurts of your heart. If you offer them to your loving Savior, they will not be wasted. They will never be for nothing. They are a testimony to you of who God is, and they can now be a testimony to others of who God can be in *their* lives as well.

STEP #10 *Toward Healing and Wholeness*
Reinvest in the lives of others.
Let God turn your pain into your purpose
by offering to others hope where you once felt only hurt.

LET THE INVESTING BEGIN

1. In her book *Dear Abba*, author Claire Cloninger paints this illustration of what Christ did for us and expects us to do for others:

    See yourself ragged and hungry and locked in a prison cell on a long hallway of other cells, each one housing another ragged prisoner. Jesus is walking down the hallway. He stops at your cell and takes a large brass key from the pocket of his robe. He unlocks your cell door. He gives you food and clean clothes, then, placing the key in your hands, he instructs you to unlock the other prisoners and set them free.[8]

    What is your response to Jesus' instruction to take the key and set others free?

2. Read the following passages of Scripture and indicate, next to each reference, what God might be telling you, from His Word, about the plans He has for you to be a blessing to others:

   2 Corinthians 1:3-5—

   Ephesians 2:10—

   Philippians 4:13—

   Colossians 1:10—

3. In chapter 1, I asked you to fill in a chart of your pain and the praise you could offer to God in spite of it. Now I want you to revisit that chart and think about what God has shown you in your pain (or allowed you to go through) and what you can now offer to others as a result of what Christ has done in and through your life. (I completed the first one for you.)

What God Has Shown Me Through My Pain:	What I Can Now Offer to Others:
He is the only One who can meet the deep desires of my heart.	My personal testimony of looking to God as my spiritual Husband and finding He is the only One who satisfies.

A Prayer for Passing It On

Redeeming and Restoring Lord,
You had Your glory in mind when You allowed my life's
circumstances to roll out as they have. Don't let me think for
a minute that any pain or pleasure in my life has ever been
for me to keep for myself. You desire that I offer it all up to
You so You can redeem it and restore it into something beau-
tiful in my life and to benefit the lives of others. How won-
drous that You can take what was once bitter in my life and
turn it into a blessing—something that can instill hope and
courage in someone else.

Thank You, precious Lord, for reaching down from on high
and taking hold of me and drawing me out of deep waters.
Thank You for bringing me out into a spacious place where I
can breathe again and dance again and live lightly and freely.
Thank You for rescuing me because You "delighted in me."[9]
May You delight in me further as I pass on to others the hope
and healing You have given me.

A Parting Challenge: Embracing Wholeness

"Embrace this God-life. Really embrace it,
and nothing will be too much for you."

—JESUS (MARK 11:22 MSG)

When you started this journey, perhaps you were feeling some pain in your heart and wondering why God might've allowed it and what He might be able to do with it. And prayerfully, by now you are realizing God had a reason for what He allowed, He has built a stronger character in you through it all, and He intends to be glorified through the hope and healing He has accomplished in you.

It's been said, "God don't make no junk." But I also believe God won't waste a wound. He specializes in redeeming and restoring and recreating those He loves into masterpieces for His glory.[1] But that will only happen as you walk out of your place of pain and into the place of wholeness where you live daily according to the new identity He has given you.

In closing, I want to share with you a happy ending that is really a new beginning.

Sharon, the wounded little girl in chapter 2, was able to write this on one of the last pages of her journal as she worked through the years of horrific abuse she endured. It is a testimony to who God is and how He has equipped her to be the woman He designed—a woman who can now invest in the lives of others. My hope is that you'll see that her "happy ending" is just the start of a new life of joy:

> As she looks in the mirror at the once-invisible and broken woman, she finally sees the treasure God created her to be.
>
> All the years of tears, shattered dreams, and an empty heart have been healed.
>
> How? She does not know. When? She wishes she could say on a certain day...
>
> But the Lord healed her a little bit at a time. He guarded her fragile spirit and each day gave her a small amount of courage, strength, and wisdom.
>
> He sent angels to sit with her in the darkness, He provided children to teach her to laugh again, and He gave her words and actions to stop people from hurting her.
>
> He gave her a warm, secure place to feel fear, cry tears of grief, scream and search for a loving God, the one of her dreams. Most of all, He gave her time to heal all the shattered years.
>
> One day the life that owned her was fading and a new life was beginning.
>
> Yes, beginning. She may feel older, but her spirit is so very young again...just where it needs to be.
>
> She embraces life today; it no longer has monsters that lurk in the darkness.
>
> Does she feel blessed today? Yes! Why? Because of Jesus' love for her. When she could not see, feel, or trust Him, He never gave up on her.
>
> She praises her God for her life. All of it. The incest, the murder, the divorces, the cancer, the beatings. The utter despair.
>
> She knows where she's been. She knows who she has

become. At last, she has grown into the woman God designed her to be.

She has many gifts: she loves with all her heart, she has a heart full of forgiveness, she has patience and self-control; she is nurturing, she has humor, she has a positive attitude, and she allows others the privilege of being themselves.

How blessed is this woman! God calls her His child. Today, she knows she is.

Dwelling in His Presence

Sharon no longer identifies herself as the hurt little girl, but the healed woman of God. She experienced God's healing as she opened her heart to who He is and invited His peace and presence to sweep through her.

You can experience His healing too as you embrace the wholeness that He has made possible at the cross, and as you celebrate life in His presence.

David the psalmist sang:

> You will make known to me the path of life;
> *In Your presence is fullness of joy;*
> In Your right hand there are pleasures forever
> (Psalm 16:11 NASB, emphasis added).

And 1 Chronicles 16:27 tells us, "Strength and joy are in His dwelling place" (NIV).

Do you too want to experience strength and joy? Then live boldly in His presence. Invite His light into the dark areas of your life. Experience His peace that comes through knowing and loving Him. And watch your life have a resounding effect on others as you find yourself among the women who are wounded no more!

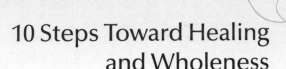

10 Steps Toward Healing and Wholeness

1. **Realize there's a reason—and a purpose—behind your pain.**
   And God's purposes are so much bigger and better than your own.

2. **Reshape your understanding of God through the Scriptures.**
   The true God of the Scriptures may be very different than the god you have perceived in your pain.

3. **Reject the lie that God doesn't care about the hurt you've experienced.**
   God has always been there and always will be. He cares. And He is still working His purposes in your life.

4. **Re-examine—and receive—the healing power of Jesus' death for you on the cross.**
   Jesus' sacrificial death was enough to heal the very deepest of your wounds—including the self-inflicted ones.

5. **Renew your mind to think differently.**
   You have a new identity in Christ—and the old you that was "just that way" is gone.

6. **Relinquish your right to yourself.**

    True surrender means recognizing your life is not your own; you belong to a loving Master who has your best at heart.

7. **Recognize the difference between real and distorted love.**

    And embrace God's love as the only love that will satisfy.

8. **Release your offender—and yourself—through forgiveness.**

    Freedom comes through letting the other person off of your emotional hook.

9. **Refresh your soul by praising God in your pain.**

    Becoming grateful to God in everything is the primary way to live out God's will for you.

10. **Reinvest in the lives of others.**

    Let God turn your pain into your purpose by offering to others hope where you once felt only hurt.

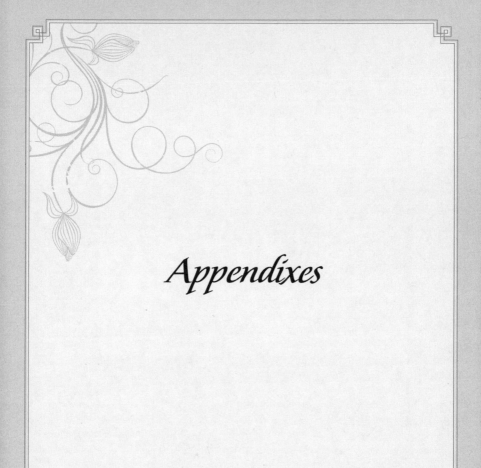

Appendixes

Appendix A:

Self-Assessment: Are You Still Affected by Your Wounds?

A nswer *yes* to the statements you believe describe yourself and *no* to the ones that don't apply. The more truthful you are with yourself, the more quickly you will be able to address your wounds and move past some of life's hurts.

When I meet someone, I tend to assume
they won't like me . . . . Yes / No

I tend to be suspicious of my husband or boyfriend,
without reason . . . . Yes / No

I avoid crowds . . . . Yes / No

I regularly lose sleep thinking about things
someone said or did to me . . . . Yes / No

I am bitter when I think about my parent(s). . . . . Yes / No

I avoid being alone. It makes me feel uncomfortable . . . . . Yes / No

I am afraid to be myself around others . . . . Yes / No

I feel uncomfortable when someone notices me . . . . Yes / No

I experience moments when I wish I wasn't alive . . . . Yes / No

I fear failure if I try something new. . . . . Yes / No

I feel frightened or depressed when I'm alone . . . . Yes / No

I cry easily . . . . Yes / No

I tend to crave the attention of others. . . . . Yes / No

I am consumed by worry . . . . Yes / No

I often feel like a little girl. . . . . Yes / No

There are times when I am consumed by fear . . . . Yes / No

The mention of God or church makes me uncomfortable . . . Yes / No

I fear not measuring up to others' expectations. . . . . Yes / No

I feel that my husband, children, and/or family
would be better off without me . . . . Yes / No

I haven't cried in years . . . . Yes / No

I feel hatred toward myself. . . . . Yes / No

I do not believe I can be completely forgiven . . . . Yes / No

I am distrustful or suspicious of people I once trusted . . . . Yes / No

I have a hard time forgiving myself . . . . Yes / No

I feel that if I were to die, no one would notice or care . . . . Yes / No

I don't believe I deserve anything good that
has happened to me. . . . . Yes / No

I sometimes feel helpless. . . . . Yes / No

I tend to be controlling . . . . Yes / No

I find it difficult to make decisions . . . . Yes / No

I rely on alcohol or medication/drugs to make me
feel better emotionally . . . . Yes / No

My intimate relationships are more short-term
than long-term..................................... Yes / No

I have developed a strong dislike or possibly even
hatred toward some people .... Yes / No

I am often angry or depressed .... Yes / No

I have disturbing, recurrent dreams .... Yes / No

I find myself thinking or saying,
"I just don't feel anything." .... Yes / No

These questions are some I have used, through the years, to help identify the core issues in a woman's life. Your responses to some statements may simply represent personality quirks or the need for further spiritual growth. However, some may indicate some deeper hurts in your life.

If you have answered yes to nine or more of the questions on this list, it is very likely there are unresolved hurts in your past or present that are continuing to impact your life and behavior. There is hope, however. The Scriptural Encouragement for Hurting Hearts on the next page is one place to start. Immersing yourself in the Word of God will help you gain a correct view of God and who you are in His sight. An individual or small group study of *When a Woman Overcomes Life's Hurts* is another step you can take on the road to healing. In addition, I recommend you talk to a pastor or trusted friend about biblical counseling or Bible-based resources that can help you in your healing process.

Scriptural Encouragement for Hurting Hearts

Reason for Our Pain

"We know that all things work together for good to those who love God, to those who are the called according to His purpose. For whom he foreknew, He also predestined to be conformed to the image of His Son" *(Romans 8:28-29)*.

"Blessed be the God and Father of our Lord Jesus Christ, the Father of mercies and God of all comfort, who comforts us in all our tribulation, that we may be able to comfort those who are in any trouble, with the comfort with which we ourselves are comforted by God" *(2 Corinthians 1:3-4)*.

"My brethren, count it all joy when you fall into various trials, knowing that the testing of your faith produces patience. But let patience have its perfect work, that you may be perfect and complete, lacking nothing" *(James 1:2-4)*.

God's Purpose/Sovereignty

"As for you, you meant evil against me; but God meant it for good" *(Genesis 50:20)*.

"'My thoughts are not your thoughts nor are your ways My ways,' says the LORD. 'For as the heavens are higher than the earth, so are My ways higher than your ways, and My thoughts than your thoughts'" *(Isaiah 55:8-9).*

"The LORD gave another message to Jeremiah. He said, 'Go down to the potter's shop, and I will speak to you there.' So I did as he told me and found the potter working at his wheel. But the jar he was making did not turn out as he had hoped, so he crushed it into a lump of clay again and started over. Then the LORD gave me this message: 'O Israel, can I not do to you as this potter has done to his clay? As the clay is in the potter's hand, so are you in my hand'" *(Jeremiah 18:1-6 NLT).*

"Our light affliction, which is but for a moment, is working for us a far more exceeding and eternal weight of glory, while we do not look at the things which are seen, but at the things which are not seen. For the things which are seen are temporary, but the things which are not seen are eternal" *(2 Corinthians 4:17-18).*

Cleansing and Forgiveness

"I acknowledged my sin to You,
And my iniquity I have not hidden.
I said, 'I will confess my transgressions to the LORD,'
And You forgave the iniquity of my sin" *(Psalm 32:5).*

"Have mercy upon me, O God,
According to Your lovingkindness;
According to the multitude of Your tender mercies,
Blot out my transgressions.
Wash me thoroughly from my iniquity,
And cleanse me from my sin" *(Psalm 51:1-2).*

"As far as the east is from the west,
So far has He removed our transgressions from us" *(Psalm 103:12).*

"Search me, O God, and know my heart;
Try me and know my anxieties;
And see if there is any wicked way in me,
And lead me in the way everlasting" *(Psalm 139:23-24).*

"I, even I, am He who blots out your transgressions for My own sake; and I will not remember your sins" *(Isaiah 43:25).*

"I will forgive their iniquity, and their sin I will remember no more" *(Jeremiah 31:34).*

"He will again have compassion on us; and will subdue our iniquities. You will cast out all our sins into the depths of the sea" *(Micah 7:19).*

"As the elect of God, holy and beloved, put on tender mercies, kindness, humility, meekness, longsuffering; bearing with one another, and forgiving one another, if anyone has a complaint against another; even as Christ forgave you, so you also must do" *(Colossians 3:12-13).*

"If we confess our sins, He is faithful and just to forgive us our sins and to cleanse us from all unrighteousness" *(1 John 1:9).*

Comfort and Deliverance

"I will both lie down in peace, and sleep;
For You alone, O Lord, make me dwell in safety" *(Psalm 4:8).*

"His anger is but for a moment,
His favor is for life;
Weeping may endure for a night,
But joy comes in the morning" *(Psalm 30:5).*

"You are my hiding place;
You shall preserve me from trouble;
You shall surround me with songs of deliverance" *(Psalm 32:7).*

"I waited patiently for the LORD;
And He inclined to me,
And heard my cry.
 He also brought me up out of a horrible pit,
Out of the miry clay,
And set my feet upon a rock,
And established my steps.
 He has put a new song in my mouth—
Praise to our God;
Many will see it and fear,
And will trust in the LORD" *(Psalm 40:1-3)*.

"God is our refuge and strength,
A very present help in trouble.
Therefore we will not fear,
Even though the earth be removed,
And though the mountains be carried into the midst of the sea;
Though its waters roar and be troubled,
Though the mountains shake with its swelling" *(Psalm 46:1-3)*.

"Trust in Him at all times, you people;
Pour out your heart before Him;
God is a refuge for us" *(Psalm 62:8)*.

"My help comes from the LORD,
Who made heaven and earth.
He will not allow your foot to be moved;
He who keeps you will not slumber"
(Psalm 121:2-3).

"Where can I go from Your Spirit?
Or where can I flee from Your presence?
If I ascend into heaven, You are there;
If I make my bed in hell, behold, You are there.
If I take the wings of the morning,

And dwell in the uttermost parts of the sea,
Even there Your hand shall lead me,
And Your right hand shall hold me.
If I say, 'Surely the darkness shall fall on me,'
Even the night shall be light about me;
Indeed, the darkness shall not hide from You,
But the night shines as the day;
The darkness and the light are both alike to You" *(Psalm 139:7-12).*

"The LORD is gracious and full of compassion,
Slow to anger and great in mercy.
The LORD is good to all,
And His tender mercies are over all His works" *(Psalm 145:8-9).*

"When you pass through the waters, I will be with you;
And through the rivers, they shall not overflow you.
When you walk through the fire, you shall not be burned,
Nor shall the flame scorch you" *(Isaiah 43:2).*

"'I know the thoughts that I think toward you,' says the LORD, 'thoughts of peace and not of evil, to give you a future and a hope'" *(Jeremiah 29:11).*

"The LORD has appeared of old to me, saying: 'Yes, I have loved you with an everlasting love; Therefore with lovingkindness I have drawn you'" *(Jeremiah 31:3).*

"I am convinced that nothing can ever separate us from God's love. Neither death nor life, neither angels nor demons, neither our fears for today nor our worries about tomorrow—not even the powers of hell can separate us from God's love. No power in the sky above or in the earth below—indeed, nothing in all creation will ever be able to separate us from the love of God that is revealed in Christ Jesus our LORD" *(Romans 8:38-39 NLT).*

"Blessed be the God and Father of our Lord Jesus Christ, the Father of mercies and God of all comfort, who comforts us in all our tribulation, that we may be able to comfort those who are in any trouble, with the comfort with which we ourselves are comforted by God" *(Hebrews 13:5).*

"He Himself has said, 'I will never leave you nor forsake you'" *(2 Corinthians 1:3-4).*

Comfort in the Face of Death

"Even though I walk through the valley of the shadow of death,
    I will fear no evil,
for you are with me;
    your rod and your staff,
    they comfort me" *(Psalm 23:4 ESV).*

"Precious in the sight of the LORD
Is the death of His saints" *(Psalm 116:15).*

"Jesus said to her, 'I am the resurrection and the life. He who believes in Me, though he may die, he shall live. And whoever lives and believes in Me shall never die'" *(John 11:25-26).*

"If I go and prepare a place for you, I will come again and receive you to Myself; that where I am, there you may be also" *(John 14:3).*

God's Provision

"The young lions lack and suffer hunger;
But those who seek the LORD shall not lack any good thing"
(Psalm 34:10).

"The LORD God is a sun and shield;
The LORD will give grace and glory;

No good thing will He withhold
From those who walk uprightly" *(Psalm 84:11).*

"The LORD upholds all who fall,
And raises up all who are bowed down.
The eyes of all look expectantly to You,
And You give them their food in due season.
 You open Your hand
And satisfy the desire of every living thing" *(Psalm 145:14-16).*

"My God shall supply all your need according to His riches in glory
by Christ Jesus" *(Philippians 4:19).*

Healing

"He heals the brokenhearted and binds up their wounds"
(Psalm 147:3).

"Surely he has borne our griefs
And carried our sorrows;
Yet we esteemed Him stricken,
Smitten by God, and afflicted.
But He was wounded for our transgressions,
He was bruised for our iniquities;
The chastisement for our peace was upon Him,
And by His stripes we are healed" *(Isaiah 53:4-5).*

"The Spirit of the LORD is upon Me,
Because He has anointed Me
To preach the gospel to the poor;
He has sent Me to heal the brokenhearted,
To proclaim liberty to the captives
And recovery of sight to the blind
To set at liberty those who are oppressed" *(Luke 4:18).*

Restoration

"Create in me a clean heart, O God,
And renew a steadfast spirit within me.
Do not cast me away from Your presence,
And do not take Your Holy Spirit from me.
Restore to me the joy of Your salvation,
And uphold me by Your generous Spirit"
(Psalm 51:10-12).

"I will give you a new heart and put a new spirit within you; I will
take the heart of stone out of your flesh and give you a heart of flesh"
(Ezekiel 36:26).

"Anyone who belongs to Christ has become a new person. The old life
is gone; a new life has begun!" *(2 Corinthians 5:17 NLT).*

"I have been crucified with Christ; it is no longer I who live, but
Christ lives in me; and the life which I now live in the flesh I live
by faith in the Son of God, who loved me and gave Himself for me"
(Galatians 2:20).

Significance

"You number my wanderings;
Put my tears into Your bottle;
Are they not in Your book?" *(Psalm 56:8).*

"You formed my inward parts;
You covered me in my mother's womb.
I will praise You, for I am fearfully and wonderfully made;
Marvelous are Your works,
And that my soul knows very well.
My frame was not hidden from You,
When I was made in secret,
And skillfully wrought in the lowest parts of the earth.

Your eyes saw my substance, being yet unformed.
And in Your book they all were written,
The days fashioned for me,
When as yet there were none of them.
How precious also are Your thoughts to me, O God!
How great is the sum of them!
If I should count them, they would be more in number than the sand;
When I awake, I am still with You" *(Psalm 139:13-18)*.

"Can a woman forget her nursing child,
And not have compassion on the son of her womb?
Surely they may forget,
Yet I will not forget you.
See, I have inscribed you on the palms of My hands;
Your walls are continually before Me" *(Isaiah 49:15-16)*.

"Are not two sparrows sold for a copper coin? And not one of them
falls to the ground apart from your Father's will. But the very hairs of
your head are all numbered. Do not fear therefore; you are of more
value than many sparrows" *(Matthew 10:29-31)*.

Spiritual Strength

"The weapons we fight with are not the weapons of the world. On
the contrary, they have divine power to demolish strongholds. We
demolish arguments and every pretension that sets itself up against
the knowledge of God, and we take captive every thought to make it
obedient to Christ" *(2 Corinthians 10:4-5 NLT)*.

"Now to Him who is able to do exceedingly abundantly above all
that we ask or think, according to the power that works in us"
(Ephesians 3:20).

"Be strong in the Lord and in the power of His might. Put on the
whole armor of God, that you may be able to stand against the

wiles of the devil. For we do not wrestle against flesh and blood, but against principalities, against powers, against the rulers of the darkness of this age, against spiritual hosts of wickedness in the heavenly places. Therefore take up the whole armor of God, that you may be able to withstand in the evil day, and having done all, to stand. Stand therefore, having girded your waist with truth, having put on the breastplate of righteousness, and having shod your feet with the preparation of the gospel of peace; above all, taking the shield of faith with which you will be able to quench all the fiery darts of the wicked one. And take the helmet of salvation, and the sword of the Spirit, which is the word of God; praying always with all prayer and supplication in the Spirit, being watchful to this end with all perseverance and supplication for all the saints" *(Ephesians 6:10-18).*

"Be anxious for nothing, but in everything by prayer and supplication, with thanksgiving, let your requests be made known to God; and the peace of God, which surpasses all understanding, will guard your hearts and minds through Christ Jesus" *(Philippians 4:6-7).*

"Whatever is true, whatever is noble, whatever is right, whatever is pure, whatever is lovely whatever is admirable—if anything is excellent or praiseworthy—think about such things" *(Philippians 4:8 NIV).*

"I can do all things through Christ who strengthens me" *(Philippians 4:13).*

Suggestions for Planning and Facilitating a Small-group Study

Healing often happens in community, as women transparently share their hearts with one another, pray for and receive prayer from one another, and have someone to hold them accountable for their healing and spiritual growth and health.

With the help of this book, one of the best ways to help facilitate healing to others is to lead (or recommend that a leader in your church lead) a women's small-group study. The application questions, Bible study, and prayers included at the end of each chapter were designed for both individual and group use.

Here is how you or someone you know can start and lead a small group study of *When a Woman Overcomes Life's Hurts*:

Preparing to Start the Group

1. Pray in advance about which women would benefit from a study of this book.

2. Send out handwritten or email invitations or make personal phone calls and invite these women to come together and meet as a group.

3. Continue to pray for each woman whom you have invited to be a part of the group.

4. Give each participant a copy of the book. Have the women read a chapter each week and encourage them to come

prepared to discuss the questions at the end of that week's chapter.

5. Print out a schedule with the dates and chapters to be studied. This will help participants to stay on track in case they miss a week or two.

6. It is most helpful for the facilitator to have read the entire book (and answered all of the application questions) before starting the group study. This way, the leader knows what's coming and can keep each meeting's discussion on topic. It will also let the reader know what is coming up in the future, in case questions arise that are better answered in future meetings.

Leading the Introductory Session

1. Welcome the women to the study. Introduce yourself as their facilitator. Have each woman introduce herself and tell the group why she is interested in taking part in this study.

2. Tell the group why you are interested in facilitating this study. Share with them what you hope to get out of it personally, as well as your goal for the women in the group. The women will only be as open and honest as you are, so be as transparent as possible.

3. Open the session in prayer.

4. Have someone read the introduction aloud as others follow along. Or, have two or three women take turns reading it.

5. Read through the book's table of contents. Ask the participants which chapters they see as most needed in their lives right now.

6. Commit to praying for each other in the areas they

indicated above. You may want to assign prayer partners for this study, or have the women voluntarily team up with another woman or two with whom they can pray each week.

Leading Subsequent Sessions

While getting through the material is important, it is vital that these women know they are loved, being listened to, and in a safe environment where they can heal and come face-to-face with the Healer of their hurts. Be flexible—it's possible the group will need two or three weeks to work through a chapter. Be sensitive to the Spirit's leading, and watch for women who need extra time to process the issues they are addressing in their lives. Above all, be blessed as you bless others through leading them to the Healer of their hurts.

And if you have the opportunity, I would love to hear from you about how God works through your time together.

Cindi

Notes

Chapter 1—This Wasn't Supposed to Happen

1. Oswald Chambers, *My Utmost for His Highest,* updated edition, James Reimann, ed. (Grand Rapids: Discovery House, 1992), August 5.

2. Deuteronomy 32:4 comforts us with this assurance: "He is the Rock, his works are perfect, and all his ways are just. A faithful God who does no wrong, upright and just is he" (NIV).

3. This story is found in Genesis 37, 39–50.

4. Chambers, *My Utmost for His Highest,* June 25.

5. First Samuel 15:22 says "to obey is better than sacrifice," and Hebrews 11:6 tells us "without faith it is impossible to please Him."

Chapter 2—Why Did I Have to Hurt Like This?

1. For more information on A Path to Life Wellness Center, see www.APathtoLife.org.

Chapter 3—Where Was God, Anyway?

1. The Hebrew word for "searched" means to "intimately examine," E-Sword Version 10.0.5, © 2000-2012 by Rick Meyers, www.e-sword.net.

2. The Hebrew word translated "hedges" is a word meaning "to confine, hold you close, hem you in so you are safe," E-Sword Version 10.0.5.

Chapter 4—I'll Never Be Completely Healed

1. Second Samuel 23:8-39 lists David's mighty men, and Uriah the Hittite is the last one mentioned, a subtle tribute to the man whom David had betrayed.

2. This story is recorded in 2 Samuel 11.

3. This account is told in 2 Samuel 12 and God's statement to David, through the prophet Nathan, appears in verse 8.

4. All these word studies were conducted using E-Sword Version 10.0.5.

5. Nancy Leigh DeMoss, *Lies Women Believe and the Truth that Sets Them Free* (Chicago: Moody, 2001), p. 209.

Chapter 5—That's Just the Way I Am

1. Natasha and I both caution readers when it comes to depending on dreams to hear the voice of God. Because our subconscious thoughts play such a heavy role in our dream process, frequently we're hearing our own thoughts rather than God. However, because this dream did not contradict Scripture, but reinforced to Natasha a passage she remembered in Psalm 23:5, she believes God used this dream to reaffirm a biblical truth to her and speak to her in a way that she might not have otherwise listened to or understood.

2. John MacArthur, *Twelve Extraordinary Women* (Nashville, TN: Thomas Nelson, 2005), p. 176 (emphasis added).

Chapter 6—I Have a Right to Be Happy

1. Jill Kelly, *Without a Word* (New York: Faith Words, 2010), p. 92.

2. Kelly, *Without a Word*, p. 178.

3. Kelly, *Without a Word*, p. 201.

4. For more information or to contribute, visit www.huntershope.org.

5. John MacArthur, *Slave: The Hidden Truth About Your Identity in Christ* (Nashville, TN: Thomas Nelson, 2010), p. 12.

6. MacArthur, *Slave*, p. 17.

7. NASB.

8. Kelly, *Without a Word*, p. 119.

9. Oswald Chambers, *My Utmost for His Highest*, updated edition, James Reimann, ed. (Grand Rapids: Discovery House, 1992), August 31.

10. Jill Kelly, *Prayers of Hope for the Brokenhearted* (Eugene, OR: Harvest House, 2010), pp. 13-14. Used with permission.

Chapter 7—I'll Never Really Be Loved

1. For more on letting God fill the hunger in your heart, see my book *Letting God Meet Your Emotional Needs*, available at www.StrengthForTheSoul.com.

2. Revelation 2:5 NIV.

3. E-Sword Version 10.0.5, © 2000-2012 by Rick Meyers.

Chapter 8—I Can Finally Be Free

1. Emergency Marriage Seminar is run by Rick Reynolds of Affair Recovery. For more information see www.affairrecovery.com.

2. Matthew 6:14-15.

3. Genesis 50:19-20 NASB.

4. Robert Jeffress, *Say Goodbye to Regret* (Sisters, OR: Multnomah, 1998), p. 148.

5. Jeffress, *Say Goodbye to Regret*, p. 148.

6. Jeffress, *Say Goodbye to Regret*.

7. This suggested prayer is part of "Lesson 2: Fellowship with God" in the *Knowing God Personally* curriculum published by Multiplication Ministries, © 1996.

Chapter 9—I Can Experience Joy Again

1. *The Joy of the Lord Is My Strength* by Cyndi Evans, © 2009. Used with permission.

2. A good place to start studying the names and character of God is my book *When God Pursues a Woman's Heart* (Eugene, OR: Harvest House Publishers, 2003). The book is available at www.StrengthForTheSoul.com.

3. NASB.

4. NASB.

Chapter 10—I Can Be a Blessing

1. For more information on Holding Out HELP, see the organization's website at www.holdingouthelp.org or call 801-548-3492; or write 12300 S. 138 E. Ste. C #193, Draper, UT 84020.

2. For more information about this ministry or to find out how you can help, or to read Misty's story in its entirety, see www.youareajewel.org.

3. Ephesians 6:16 NIV.

4. Oswald Chambers, *My Utmost for His Highest*, updated edition, James Reimann, ed. (Grand Rapids: Discovery House, 1992), June 8.

5. Cyndi Evans, "Release" © 2009; used with permission.

6. Oswald Chambers, *My Utmost for His Highest*, September 6.

7. Oswald Chambers, *My Utmost for His Highest*, September 9.

8. Claire Cloninger, *Dear Abba: Finding the Father's Heart Through Prayer* (Dallas: Word, 1997), p. 117.

9. A portion of this prayer was taken from Psalm 18:16-19 (NIV).

A Parting Challenge: Embracing Wholeness

1. In the New Living Translation, Ephesians 2:10 says, "We are God's masterpiece. He has created us anew in Christ Jesus, so that we can do the good things he planned for us long ago."

An Invitation to Write

Where has God met you on your journey toward healing and wholeness as you've read through this book? Cindi would love to hear from you and know how you've been ministered to or encouraged through her writing.

You can contact her online at
Cindi@StrengthForTheSoul.com

Or you can write:
Cindi McMenamin
c/o Harvest House Publishers
990 Owen Loop North
Eugene, OR 97402-9173

If you would like to have Cindi speak to your group, you can find more information about her speaking ministry at www.StrengthForTheSoul.com.